Figure Skating School

Figure Skating School

A PROFESSIONALLY STRUCTURED COURSE FROM BASIC STEPS
TO ADVANCED TECHNIQUES

PETER MORRISSEY AND JAMES YOUNG

FIREFLY BOOKS

A FIREFLY BOOK

First published in Canada in 1997 by
Firefly Books Ltd.
3680 Victoria Park Avenue
Willowdale, Ontario M2H 3KI

First published in the U.S. in 1997 by
Firefly Books (U.S.) Inc.
P.O. Box 1338, Ellicott Station
Buffalo, New York 14205

Cataloguing in Publication Data

Young, James, 1946
  Figure Skating School

ISBN 1-55209-166-X

I. Skating. I. Morrissey, Peter, 1953–   II. Title.
GV850.4.Y686 1997   796.91'2   C97-930881 X

Creative Director: Richard Dewing
Art Director: Clare Reynolds
Designer: Roger Fawcett-Tang
Senior Editor: Sally Green
Editor: Andrew Armitage
Illustrator: Julian Baker

Typeset in Great Britain by
Central Southern Typesetters, Eastbourne
Manufactured in Singapore by
United Graphics Pte Ltd.
Printed in Singapore by
Star Standard Industries (Pte) Ltd.

Contents

Introduction

Figure skating over the last 30 years has progressed in leaps and bounds both technically and artistically, which has led to it becoming one of the most popular television viewing sports throughout the world. Now millions of viewers sit avidly watching major skating events, enjoying and becoming more informed about the difficulties of this most complicated of sports. During this period skaters of World and Olympic status have gone from doing single jumps in order to win, to doing triples in combination and now even quadruple jumps in the men's event. This is all due to improved training conditions, methods and technical know-how, and it is the aim of this book to lead you in a logical way through the intricacies of modern figure skating technique, from your first steps on the ice through to building a repertoire of steps and footwork of basic skating movements, and finally to jumps and spins of the very top level of skating.

This book will take you from the very basic techniques of skating forward and backwards and guide you in looking for the correct equipment and how to ensure that it is properly used and looked after. After that you are led through all the basic turns and steps, such as chassés, runs, crosscuts, three turns, mohawks and choctaws, with details of how to perform them. Verbal explanations are accompanied by wonderful illustrations of many of the moves to help you understand what is required and the main things to be aware of when practising. This is then followed with a logical progression through the jumps: which jumps to start with and what is probably the best order for most people to follow. It must be said that you should **first master all the single jumps and then follow this with your double jumps**. It is very important that your method and technique for the single jumps is good and reliable before progressing further. Only at this point is it normal to try the doubles of those jumps you are best at, until you can do them all. Finally when you feel able, you should tackle your triples or even quads, but remember that you should always put safety first and if possible do these movements under the supervision of a coach. However it is hoped that this book will help you in more readily understanding the techniques involved at all levels, and it has been designed to be simple to use and understand.

It should be remembered that skating from beginner level to even the most elite levels should be fun, and learning new skills and developing ideas should be a pleasure. It is certainly hoped that this book will give you as much pleasure "off ice" when reading about skating as you have when skating. With this as a guide, when you attend a training or skating session you will be able to reap the full benefit of what you are trying to achieve.

SURYA BONALY DEMONSTRATES A DYNAMIC "SPLIT JUMP."

Figure Skating – a Brief History

Ice skating started as a fast means of transport during the heavy winters of Northern Europe and at first bones were used to form the skates, which were then tied onto the feet. Iron runners succeeded bone and were fastened to snowshoes or, as in Holland, to wooden slabs. Nobody really seems to know exactly when or how this all happened. However, skating really seems to have developed first in Scandinavia, from where it spread to England, Austria, Germany, Holland, and then to North America, where now it is a multimillion-dollar, high-profile sport, getting immense television coverage and exposure and resulting in many famous World and Olympic Champions.

However perhaps the first skater of real note was a Norwegian, Axel Paulsen, who was a speed skater and went on to invent the famous Axel jump. This is a one-and-a-half-revolution jump from forward outside to back outside edge – but don't let the technicalities put you off. All will be explained. Modern top skaters now do triples of three-and-a-half revolutions, which shows how far the sport has developed in the last 50 years. Ulrich Salchow of Sweden, who gave his name to the Salchow jump, was a ten times World Champion, and Gillis Grafsom, also of Sweden, was winner of three Olympic Gold Medals.

Another famous Scandinavian skater – and film star – was Sonja Henie, from Norway, who was also a ten-times World Champion and a three-times Olympic title holder. She brought modern skating to the fore and to the public's attention. Her films and ice shows made skating glamorous. Their influence sent untold hordes of children staggering over the ice. Henie was the first international celebrity in the world of figure skating and it was her skating and showmanship that did much to make skating the popular sport that it is today throughout the world.

Nowadays, figure skating is truly worldwide, with the international governing body, the International Skating Union (ISU), based in Davos, Switzerland, having some 70 member countries worldwide from such far-flung places as Japan, Korea, Australia, South Africa, the USA, Canada, and most of the European countries. Every year standards rise dramatically and now countries such as Russia, the United States, and Canada lead the way.

However, just prior to this, during the late fifties, sixties, and early seventies, Great Britain did much to help develop the fine technical skills of the sport through names like Gladys Hogg and the Gerschwilers, who in turn taught such skaters as Sjoukje Dijkstra, John Curry, and Robin Cousins – all Olympic Gold Medalists – to name but a few. Then there were such greats as Torvill and Dean, World and Olympic dance champions who were trained by Betty Callaway in the early eighties.

It was during this time that many European coaches left

WORLD FAMOUS SONJA HENIE IN ATTITUDE POSE AGAINST A MOUNTAIN BACKDROP.

for America and have helped to develop the North American scene into the fantastic success that it is today, with skaters such as Peggy Fleming, Dorothy Hamill, Jill Trenary, Kurt Browning, Brian Boitano, Brian Orser, Michelle Kwan, and Todd Eldredge, to name very few. Most skating competitions of today have become a head-to-head between the superpowers of Russia and the North Americans.

We hope that this book will lead you in the right direction, by giving you some idea of what good technique is and what is involved in some of the fantastic performances you can see at championships and on TV these days. It will give you the opportunity to take your own skating techniques and ideas further.

Pair Skating

Pair skating can be the most spectacular of all the disciplines of figure skating and it can also be one of the most dangerous, so any attempt at this discipline should be well supervised by a trained and qualified coach. Pair skating combines all the elements of single skating such as side-by-side triple jumps, plus the spectacle of big overhead lifts, like the star, the platter, and the lasso. These, together with twist lifts, death spirals, pair spins and the male–female "love story," all add up to great entertainment, and are a true test of the skater's strength, nerve, and skills.

Because of the great complexity and danger involved in many pair-skating maneuvers, we have decided not to cover this discipline in any great detail, simply to state that if you are interested in pursuing this section of our sport further you should contact a professional coach. However, to give a little idea of pair skating, we will mention some of the great names involved in its development and some of the current requirements.

Again, initially Great Britain and Germany had much to do with pair-skating development, with such names as Maxi Herber and Ernst Baier, John and Jennifer Nicks, Marika Kilius and Hans Jurgen Baumler, and Winifred and Dennis Silverthorne. However, by the early 1960s, Russia was becoming the dominant force in pairs, with skaters such as Ludmilla Belousova and Oleg Protopopov, who in 1964 and 1968 were Olympic Gold Medalists and brought a new balletic elegance to pair skating. They were followed by their fellow Russians Irina Rodnina and Alexei Ulanov in 1972 and later Rodnina with her new partner, Alexander Zaitsev, in 1976 and 1980, giving her 10 World and three Olympic gold medals, together with Sonja Henie, who also won the same number of titles, making them the most famous skaters of all time. Rodnina's name is synonymous with modern pair skating, because it was she who brought true speed, daring, and athleticism to the sport. Russians

A TWIST LIFT IN ACTION.

still dominate this section of the sport, although there have been many excellent American and Canadian pairs, namely Babilonia and Gardner, who won Worlds in 1979, Underhill and Martini, and Lloyd Eisler and Isabelle Brasseur from Canada. The Russians' success has been mainly due to the work of the top coach Tarmara Moskvina from St Petersburg, who over the years has taught many World and Olympic Champions.

In competition, pairs skate two sections: first, a short program with required elements, side-by-side jumps, death spirals, and lifts; second, a long free program in which the skaters can choose their own elements in order to show off their own virtuosity under general guidelines. However, the elements that are judged are still recognizable moves with given names like Axels, twist lifts, death spirals, and so forth. Very often, for the average person, it can be difficult to understand the difference between pair skating and ice dancing. Generally it is simply the rules and regulations, the size of the lifts, and the emphasis on the way people move to the music.

AN EXCITING PAIR LIFT ABOVE THE HEAD.

Ice Dancing

For many years ice dancing was considered the poor relation of other skating disciplines and was the last to be accepted in its own right. But on its acceptance into the Olympic Games in 1976 the sport became truly one of the major sections of figure skating. Before that, ice dancers in countries other than Great Britain were usually failed pairs or single skaters, and ice dancing had the image of a recreational activity followed only by middle-aged skaters.

However, today this attitude has completely altered and most people now realize that ice dancing is among the most demanding of skating disciplines, giving drama, grace, romance, and glamor to the sport. This – combined with athletic lifts and with the emphasis on intricate footwork, musicality, and original choreography – has made ice dancing one of the easiest of the disciplines for the public to relate to.

British skaters have, as you might expect, dominated this section from its start right through the first 20 years of its development, with names like Demmy and Westwood, Courtney Jones and June Markham, and later his new partner, Doreen Denny. Then came Bernard Ford and Diane Towler. All were World Champions for a number of years for Great Britain.

However, from 1970 the Russians came onto the scene with Ludmilla Pakhomova and Alexander Gorshkov winning World Gold for the next six years. They brought a new emphasis on choreography, total-body movement, and drama, in true Russian style, away from the rather formal style – but good technique – of the British dancers, with their emphasis on intricate and difficult footwork.

This continued until 1981 when Great Britain, with Torvill and Dean, burst onto the scene, giving the best of both schools, with excellent technique in compulsory dances plus original choreography and a new dimension in unison. This culminated in their Olympic-Gold-winning "Bolero" free dance, which made Torvill and Dean and ice dancing household words throughout the world.

Nowadays, ice dancing, with its easily understandable boy–girl love-story relationship in many different dance rhythms and styles has made it probably the most popular event at World and Olympic events.

The biggest difference between ice dancing and pair skating is that pairs contains all of the elements of single skating, such as jumps skated side-by-side plus overhead lifts, which are set, such as Platter, Lasso, and Star. However, in ice dancing the emphasis is on difficult footwork, timing, and expression to the music, and quality of movement and skating. While dancers are allowed to lift, these are not prescribed or recognized lifts, but are original to each skater and the lifts are not allowed to go above the shoulder of the man.

The music chosen by dancers for the free section must also be "dance music" with a beat and melody, whereas pair skaters may choose any music without restriction.

Mention should also be given to the "Compulsory Dance" section, which is one of three sections skated in skating competition, where the steps, timing, holds, and patterns are laid down by the governing body, the International Skating Union. This really can be seen as comparable to ballroom dancing and is the most disciplined section. The second section is the "Original Set Pattern Dance," in which the dancers make up their own choreography and steps to a set dance rhythm. And finally they skate the "Free Dance," which includes small lifts and jumps – and it is this section that is normally seen on television.

RENÉE ROCA AND GORSHA SUR IN A DRAMATIC DANCE LIFT – BEAUTY, SKILL, AND BALANCE COMBINED.

Equipment, Safety & Coaching

The main thing to consider when you make your first visit to an ice rink or arena is how warm or cold it is, and to dress accordingly. In most cases, this will mean that you will need warm, comfortable clothing that will give you freedom of movement, at the same time keeping your muscles warm and therefore more efficient. It is important to ensure that you are well warmed up before exercising, particularly so in the generally cold conditions of an ice rink. You should spent at least 15 minutes working all your muscle groups gently prior to any physical exercise; subsequently any kind of movement will become much easier to perform as your joints will all move more freely. This will also help with your flexibility. At the end of a physically demanding training session, you should always cool down with gentle stretching exercises, which will help remove lactic acid from your muscles and alleviate unwanted aching after workouts.

The warm clothing should include slacks or trousers that allow easy movement, particularly when you are a beginner, since this will prevent grazing or cuts should you fall. Then you need warm sweaters or layers of clothing that you can remove as you become warm. Gloves are also often very useful both for warmth and for protecting your hands if you fall during a crowded session. Leg warmers can also be a help in keeping muscles warm. The basic rule is dress to keep warm, and in layers you can peel off as necessary.

Before buying your own skates it is recommended that you try skating in rented skates, just to see if you take to skating. When renting boots, always make sure that they are the correct size; never have boots that are too big as this will cause blisters, etc. Also check that the blades are sharp before skating. If they are not, ask the assistant for a sharper pair. Blunt blades and badly fitting boots can make your first visit to an ice rink a disaster.

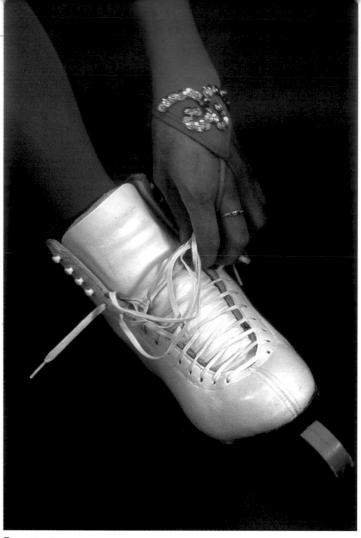

BLUNT BLADES AND BADLY-FITTING BOOTS CAN MAKE YOUR FIRST VISIT TO AN ICE RINK A DISASTER.

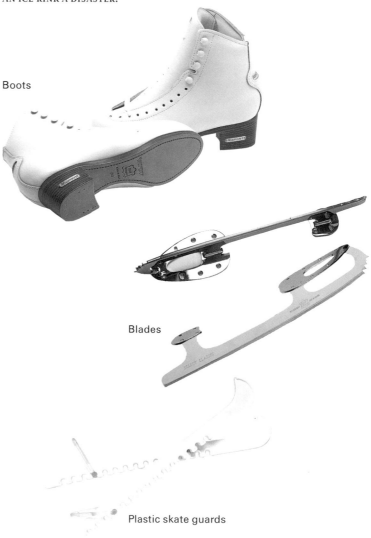

Boots

Blades

Plastic skate guards

YOUR BOOTS SHOULD FIT EXACTLY FROM HEEL TO TOE IF YOU ARE TO SKATE IN COMFORT.

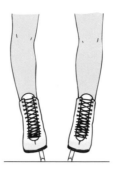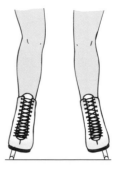

Incorrect setting of blade. Blade set too far in and foot falls to outside.

Incorrect setting of blade. Blades set too far out and foot falls to inside.

Correct setting with foot standing naturally upright.

For your first visit select a session that will suit your needs. It is a good idea to telephone the rink first and choose a session that will suit the first-time skater; quiet, and not full of fast skaters and loud music.

Once you have decided that figure skating is for you, then it is highly recommended that you purchase your own boots and skates. Your choice is vitally important, so try to get advice from an expert such as a coach. The main thing is equipment that fits well, not how expensive it is. Usually girls will wear white boots and boys black, but you should check that the boots fit exactly from heel to toe and that your foot does not move around on its own at all. The heel of the boot should fit very firmly around the ankle, because this is where you almost steer your foot around curves and turns. To this end you should tie boots tightly, particularly at the ankle area. New boots can be difficult to break in. They're not very comfortable when they are new and should not be worn for very long periods at first. It is a good idea to wear them at home, with the blades mounted and skate guards on, while watching the TV or doing odd jobs. This can help to break them in, but remember that new boots will not automatically make you a better skater. Often you will feel a lot worse before things get better.

The next important thing is to make sure that the blades are fitted correctly onto your boots. This means that they should be set directly under the physical center. This is usually from the gap between your big toe and the toe next to it and the center of your heel. This can vary from person to person and on the shape of your legs and other considerations, but to get it correct is very important if the blades are to run truly across the ice without pulling. Often the best way to feel this is to try to skate in a straight line and change your weight from heel to ball of your foot and see if they pull or travel more in one direction than the other, then to adjust them accordingly. The blade should also fit from the toe to within a half inch of the heel of the boot. As you improve, there are slightly different blades for single free skating, ice dancing, and precision or figures, but first choose all-round, good quality blades and try to ensure that they are well sharpened about every couple of months when you skate regularly. Remember that it is not the boots or the blades that make the champion but the talent and the dedication of the skater.

After skating you should make sure that your blades are wiped clean and dry. If walking around the rink off the ice, it is a good idea to wear a plastic skate guard to protect the blades from being chipped and damaged. However, make sure that you remove them before stepping onto the ice, otherwise you will have a painful experience as your feet slide away out of control and you end up in a dishevelled heap on the floor.

Safety while skating is paramount. The ice is very hard and cold, the blades sharp. A good coach is very important for your wellbeing on the ice and for all future improvement. A coach is a person who can communicate instructions to his or her pupils in a very positive and easy-to-understand manner. The coach will be there to give information on every aspect of skating. He or she will be more than a teacher, and will play many roles in making you a better skater. A good coach might not have been a champion skater themselves but will have the ability to pass on information and to see mistakes and correct them quickly and efficiently. Not every coach suits every skater and often a skater will try several coaches before finally settling with the right one. Remember that a champion skater will spend a great deal of time with their coach and it is important that you work well together as a team.

ANOTHER PAIR OF EYES AND HANDS IS ALWAYS A HELP IN GETTING THINGS RIGHT.

General Principles of Good Skating

First you need to understand that all skating elements and steps consist of four basic edges. These are **forward outside**, **forward inside**, **backward outside**, and **backward inside**, and it is very important that you master the skating of these before attempting other difficult movements. These will be covered in detail in the next section, on **Basic Skills**, but for the time being it is only necessary that you understand that when your skating foot is inclined toward its outside you will be on an outside edge, and when your skating foot is inclined toward its inside you will be on an inside edge, either forward or backward.

You also need to understand that your blade is hollow-ground, giving you these two edges, and that your blade also has a radius – or rocker – running from toe to heel, which allows you to rock your weight from front to back of your foot/blade. This means that when you are skating forwards your weight should be on the back third of your blade and when you skate backwards it is slightly further forward on the center back section.

Toe Rake or Toe Pick. Used for toe jumps and toe stops only.

This section is used for forward take off jumps and turns.

This section is used for general skating.

This section is used for backward turns.

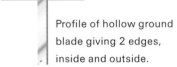

Profile of hollow ground blade giving 2 edges, inside and outside.

Note: Profile has a "rocker" or radius allowing blade and weight to change from ball to heel.

This radius is also used when turning, (see the section on **Three Turns**) or when taking off for an Axel jump. The toe picks or rakes are used only when "spotting" for toe jumps or doing toe steps. Otherwise you should avoid pushing or skating on your toe picks. This is a common fault when novice skaters start to skate backwards.

Right outside   Left outside   Right inside   Left inside

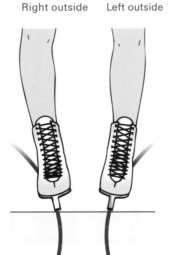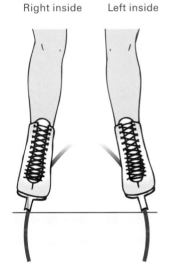

When skating outside edges your blades would move in this shape or curve/edge.

When skating inside edges your blades will move in this shape or curve.

Here are 10 basic rules that generally apply to figure skating. These are some of the most important things that you can learn and you should try to apply them to your skating at all times during your development from beginner to championship skater. It should always be worth reading this list every so often to see if you are really applying them to your skating; remember that good practice makes perfect.

1   Your hips and shoulders should remain parallel to the ice as much as possible at all times.

2   If you are skating in a straight line your hips and shoulders should be square to your line of travel.

3   When you are skating on an edge or curve – which should be almost all of the time – your hips should be offset at about 45 degrees to your line of travel, so that, when you are skating forwards, the hip innermost to the circle should be in the lead or forward, causing your hips to face to the outside of the circle you are making. When skating backwards your hips face inside the circle with your innermost hip held back and in the lead.

4   Both knees should always be bent before you push, and keep your weight on your pushing foot while you make this movement, so that you never stand on two feet at the same time – unless it is for special effect, as for instance in a spread eagle.

5   Each edge or step should continue the line of the previous edge as much as possible to help continue the flow of the movement.

6   Your skating knee should always be active, rising or falling; the skating knee should never reach the total top or bottom of the range of movement, as this will cause stops or breaks in your movement as you unlock your knee joints.

7   Your free leg should always be extended directly over the tracing of the skating foot unless otherwise required and it should be turned out with your toe pointed downward. The skating knee should work the free leg so that the skating knee is active and the free leg is passive. This means that as you rise on the skating knee the free leg is drawn in and as you bend on the skating knee the free leg is extended.

GOOD BALANCE TRAVELS IN A DIRECT LINE FROM YOUR SHOULDER THROUGH YOUR HIP, DOWN THE LINE OF YOUR SKATING LEG INTO YOUR SKATING FOOT.

8   Pushes should always be made from an inside edge, using the complete length of the blade, not using your toe pick in order to push. When stepping from backward to forward you should always step at about 90 degrees outside of the circle, not round the curve, as this causes over-rotation.

9   Good posture is very important if you are to look good on the ice, and this will always involve an upright back, which should be obtained by using your stomach muscles, not by arching your back. It should feel as if someone had hit you in your stomach so that it is held in strongly, and your pelvis is tucked under so that the buttocks are held tightly together. This will allow you to make an axis, which should go directly from your shoulder through your hip, down the line of your skating leg into your skating foot, hence giving you good balance and giving an elegant appearance.

10   Your head should always be held erect and looking over one shoulder or the other depending upon which shoulder is leading; and your arms should also be held extended and in a natural curve with your shoulders so that your hands can be seen in your peripheral vision.

First Steps

Basic Skills

The Forward Outside Edge

The first of the four basic edges to be learned is the **Forward Outside Edge**. This position can best be learned from forward chassés (see the section on Forward Chassés). Simple reduce the number of chassés until you are comfortable standing on one foot for a complete circle, without wobbling.

Your skating foot should be inclined outwards and your tracing, or skating hip should be forward or leading, so that your hips face outside of the circle by about 45 degrees, together with your shoulders. Your leading arm should be over your proposed line of skating and the other arm held extended and elegantly to the side, with your free leg extended behind you over the tracing.

When you are at ease with this then you should gently swing your free leg forward, making sure that you brush your skating foot with the heel of your free leg, just after the halfway mark of your circle. Then you can repeat this on the other foot, making sure that, as you return your free leg alongside the new skating foot, you draw your new skating hip forward, together with your arm and shoulder, in preparation for shifting your weight to the new skating hip, and thereby gaining the same position you started with – but using the other side of your body.

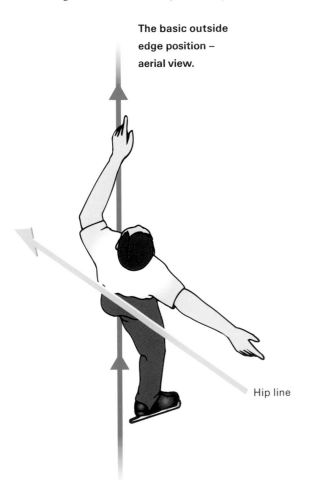

The basic outside edge position – aerial view.

Hip line

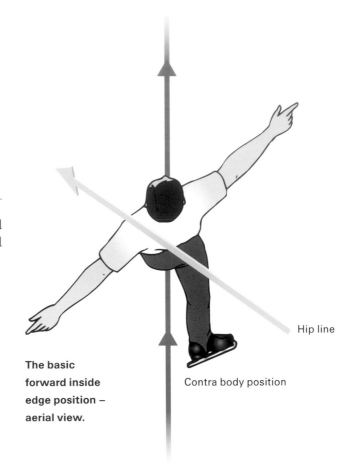

The basic forward inside edge position – aerial view.

Contra body position

Hip line

The Forward Inside Edge

This time you stand in exactly the same position but on the other foot so that, if you stand on your right foot, you have your left hip, shoulder, and arm forward and facing outside of the circle but this time you incline your foot toward the inside. These can also be started from chassés. Once again, simply reduce the number of chassés as for outsides. When you are able to maintain this position for some time, then again you simply swing your free leg forward, again brushing the skating foot in doing so. At the same time you should reverse your arms totally against your leg. This allows you to be ready to repeat the movement on the other foot.

The Backward Outside Edge

This is the next basic skill to tackle. Again this can be developed from backward chassés (see section on Backward Chassés), gradually reducing the number until you are able to hold an outside edge as long as you wish. For backward movement you will have your hips and shoulders facing about 45 degrees to the inside of the circle. For instance, if you are standing on your right foot it will be inclined toward its outside and your right hip and shoulder will be back or, as you are moving backwards, in the lead. Your right arm will be held almost over the tracing and the left arm will be held to the side and inside of the tracing or circle. Your head should be looking over your right shoulder in the direction you wish to skate. This helps to keep your weight up over the back of your right tracing hip.

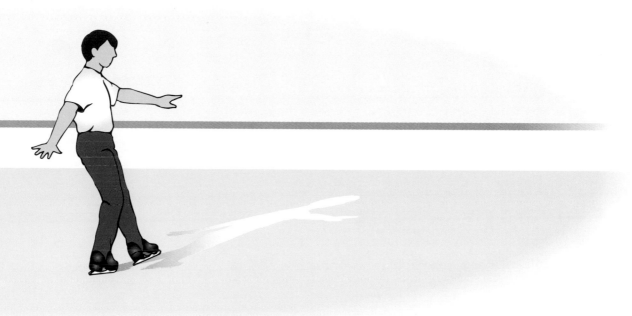

The basic back inside edge position.

When you are able to hold this for as long as you wish then you just swing your free leg gently back in one continuous movement, again brushing your free leg along your skating foot. At the same time you should rotate your hips and shoulders to the outside of the circle while keeping your left arm checked across the front of your body to stop you from over-rotating. You will feel your weight move from your right hip back to the outside of the circle over to the left hip. As your free leg starts to return toward your skating leg, you should allow your left arm to open so that you can push onto the other foot in your new basic position and repeat this on the other side.

The Backward Inside Edge

This is the last basic edge to learn. Again this can be learned from chassés but this time your skating foot will be inclined toward the inside of your foot. Your free leg should be extended in front of your body and you should be facing toward the inside of the circle, once again with your head looking in the direction you intend to skate. Then simply swing your free leg back along your skating foot until it is extended behind you. When you strike for your next circle you will find that you are looking out of the circle initially and your weight will almost feel braced against the circle over the back of your tracing hip. This is the true back inside position, and this time, as you swing your free leg, you will have to release your body to face inside of the circle and this will allow you to feel your weight change from being braced against the circle to back and *in* the circle. This should then be repeated on the other foot in this manner.

KATARINA WITT SHOWS GRACE AND POISE AS WELL AS THE IMPORTANCE OF EYE CONTACT WITH AN AUDIENCE AS A MEANS OF COMMUNICATION.

Basic Skating

Basic skating (or stroking), is like learning to play scales for a pianist. It is extremely important, for the better the quality of your basic stroking, the better skater you will become. Every training session should start and finish with just stroking around the rink, trying each time to increase speed, correctness, stance, precision, ease, and softness of movement. You can never practice this basic element too much.

Skating Forwards for the Complete Beginner

When you start skating you should simply begin by standing on both feet with your feet turned out in a V position. This is with your heels together and your toes apart. Then simply mark time by changing your weight from one foot to the other to the count of a slow one–two. When you feel comfortable doing this, your legs should be slightly bent and relaxed. Stand upright with your shoulders and hips level, arms held to the side, and your head upright and looking forward where you will skate.

You should slowly start to move each foot forward, in turn, by about half a foot's distance, so that you move your "free foot" (the foot that you are not standing on) forward to the instep of your "skating foot" (the foot on which you *are* standing). This will allow you to start moving slowly forwards. As you become more confident doing this you should increase your count for standing on each foot, from one to two and then three, so that you start to balance and glide longer and farther with every step/edge.

As your proficiency increases still further you should ensure that you start to bend both knees before changing feet and try to extend your free leg, so that it is turned out and straight behind you as shown in the illustration, **Basic Skating**.

At this point you should try to make certain that your free leg remains straight and turned out while you rise on your skating knee, so that this rising action draws your feet together. This should make the whole movement look coordinated and give you increased speed and flow.

This then further develops so that you skate on an outside edge and, as you start to bend both knees ready for the next step, you change edge to an inside, in order to allow the new stroke or push to take place. Again, the free foot should come half a step forward to allow the weight to progress to the next step and the hips to slightly change so that when on the left foot the left hip is forward and when standing on the right foot the right hip is forward. This follows on to the basic skating positions for edges, which will be dealt with a little later.

Once you have reached this stage you should then repeat this process for backward motion, so that you develop both forward and backward skating at the same time. Try not to develop a preference for skating only forward, simply because you find it easier.

9. The skating knee once more rises and draws the free leg in ready to commence another step. Note that while skating on an outside edge **you change to inside while bending your knee** ready to facilitate a push.

8. The skating knee is **now well bent** and the free leg should be **fully extended and turned out**. The free foot should be turned out and slightly pointed down.

You are now on a right outside edge. The right hip should be forward and the free leg extending.

6. Both knees bend and the right hip comes slightly forward, the left foot changes to an inside edge and turns out ready to "push" or "strike." Note that your weight is still on the left foot.

5. The feet close together, both legs are straight but relaxed, *not* stiff.

4. The skating knee is rising and drawing the free leg in while still turned out.

3. In this position the free leg is **fully extended** and turned out to the hip. The free foot should also be turned out and pointed slightly down.

2. Left hip forward, arms held to the side and parallel to the ice. The skating knee is bent and the free leg is extending.

1. Adopt a **T position** with the foot and your weight on the right, **both knees bent**, in preparation to push to a left outside edge. Left hip should be slightly forward.

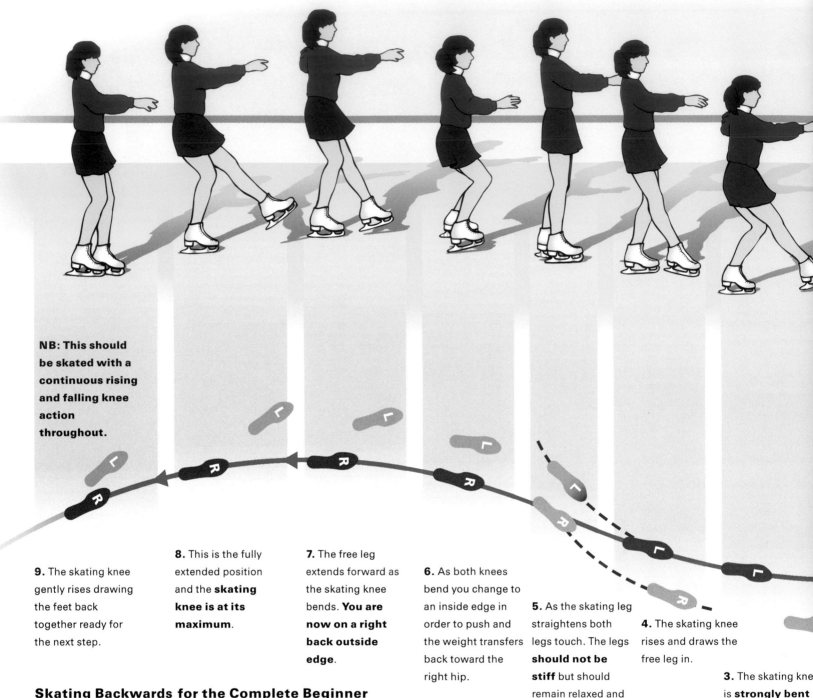

NB: This should be skated with a continuous rising and falling knee action throughout.

9. The skating knee gently rises drawing the feet back together ready for the next step.

8. This is the fully extended position and the **skating knee is at its maximum**.

7. The free leg extends forward as the skating knee bends. **You are now on a right back outside edge**.

6. As both knees bend you change to an inside edge in order to push and the weight transfers back toward the right hip.

5. As the skating leg straightens both legs touch. The legs **should not be stiff** but should remain relaxed and mobile.

4. The skating knee rises and draws the free leg in.

3. The skating knee is **strongly bent** and the free leg is extended forward and slightly turned out with the toe pointed down.

Skating Backwards for the Complete Beginner

This time you start with your feet turned in with the heels slightly apart and toes together so that you are standing with your feet in an inverted V position. Once again, you slowly shift your weight from one foot to the other, lifting one foot and then the other to a count of one and two. Then start to move one foot slightly back to the instep of your other foot. Repeat this on each foot and this will allow you to glide slowly backwards. As you gain in confidence you should increase the length of your counts to one, two, three, lifting your free leg in front of you, and as you start to glide longer on each foot make sure that your hips and shoulders are parallel to the ice and your head is upright, and once again that your arms are held out sideways.

As with forward movement, both knees should bend before pushing, and the free leg, which is extended in front of your body this time, is straight and slightly turned out,

with the toe pointed downward as shown in the illustration of backward skating.

Once again, as you improve, you should try to skate on outside edges and change to inside edges to allow the push to take place. At the same time, just as with forward stroking, you should rise on the skating knee, which will draw the feet together so that you can place the new skating foot down on the ice half a foot's distance behind the old skating foot, necessitating a slight change of hip position so that your hips will start to face the inside of the slight curve that you make. This then leads to the basic skating positions for backward motion which will be shown more clearly later.

Having mastered forward and backward skating it is time to introduce the T Stop.

The T Stop

This starts with the skater standing on one foot and gliding in a straight line. The skating leg should be bent and the position of the free leg should be as for correct forward skating, in other words extended behind and turned out at 90 degrees. The blade of the free foot is placed on the ice directly behind the skating foot. The inside edge must touch the ice and then you must keep your body weight over the skating foot until you feel the free foot touching the ice. At this point you slowly transfer your weight onto the free foot. As you do this the inside edge will drag across the ice, creating friction and bringing you to a standstill. During the stop the skating knee will rise slowly until the stop is completed. At the completion of the stop the feet will be together in a T position giving the stop its name.

This is the most "basic method" of stopping. After you can perform this with ease you could then learn snowplow and hockey stops.

ILLYA KULIK SHOWING EXCELLENT EDGE CONTROL.

1. Both feet are turned in, in a **toe-to-toe position**. Your weight should be on the right foot and the left hip is slightly back.

Both knees bend, the weight will transfer back the left hip ward the left back side edge.

The Chassé

Having developed reasonable proficiency in basic forward and backward stroking so that you can move with some ease around the rink it is now time to develop the basic positions further. For the first time the skater should start to become aware of skating on curves, and hence edges. The chassé is a series of two steps which can first be done in one direction creating a circle.

The Forward Chassé

You should commence with your left arm in front over the tracing that you intend to skate, with the left shoulder and hip slightly forward at approximately 45 degrees to your feet. The right arm should be held extended to the side with the head held upright across the left shoulder looking forward along the intended line of movement. With both knees bent and relaxed and your feet turned out in an L position (heel to heel) – and with the majority of your weight on your right foot – you should push from a right inside edge, forward onto a left forward outside edge. Your free leg should be turned out in a relaxed way from your hip, with the toe pointed and turned slightly down.

At this time you start to rise slowly and continuously on your left knee (skating knee) until it is nearly straight but still flexed. During this action your free leg is drawn in so that the skating leg is nearly straight. The feet touch together parallel to each other and also parallel to the ice with the free leg (the right foot) an inch or so above the ice. You then simply change feet or step (without any attempt to push) onto a right inside edge.

As a result of this it is not necessary to bend your skating knee, although it should be relaxed and slightly flexed. Then you bend both knees and push once again from your right inside edge onto a left outside edge. This is repeated until you have completed a circle. Throughout this movement you should keep your weight up and over your left and leading hip. You should also try to keep this movement continuous and rhythmic and we would suggest that you use the count of one, two, three.

As you improve you should try to lessen the number of chassés taken to skate a circle to one or two, increasing the time and flow of each edge. This should then be repeated on the right foot with the right hip and shoulder leading and with the left arm held to the side.

Once you are comfortable with this then you can try to skate this exercise in a serpentine shape, with one chassé on each foot so that the left hip leads on the left chassés and the right hip is drawn through to lead for the right chassés. The weight should be changed rhythmically as the leading hip changes. Please note that in this exercise you add another outside edge to the chassé to complete each half circle, so you skate outside, inside, outside, and then repeat on the next side or other foot. (The illustration shows a right forward chassé.)

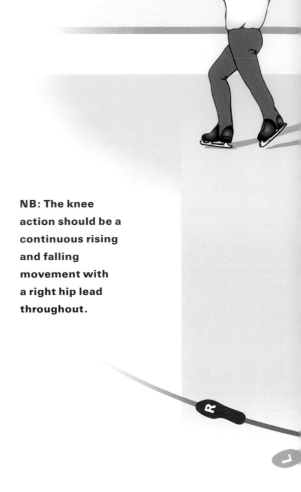

NB: The knee action should be a continuous rising and falling movement with a right hip lead throughout.

5. Again, **a basic right outside edge** – as in Figure 1.

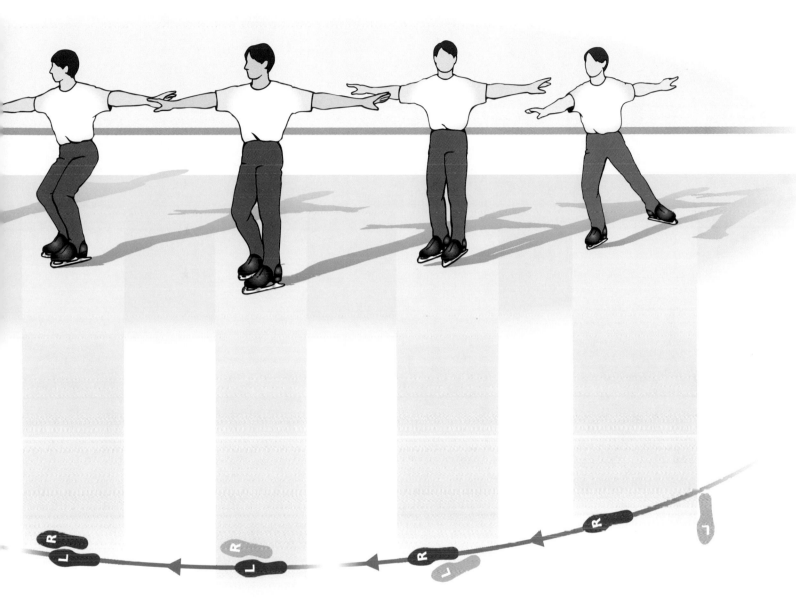

4. The same position but with **both knees strongly bent** in preparation for the push to the next step.

3. Now having changed to **a left forward inside edge**, note that the right hip and shoulder still lead and the right foot is slightly forward – the skating knee is straight but not stiff.

2. Skating knee has now risen to bring the free foot into the instep parallel to the ice, in preparation to change feet **without pushing**.

1. Basic right forward outside edge position with the right arm, hip and shoulder leading – free leg turned out and straight but not stiff – skating knee well bent.

The Backward Chassé

As with the forward chassé this can first be learned in a circle and consists of two steps: first an outside edge of two counts followed by an inside edge of one count. This time the hips face inside of the circle to be skated by about 45 degrees so that when skating in a counterclockwise direction the right hip would be back and considered to be leading. The right arm should be held back over the line that you will be skating almost directly in line with your right heel, and your head should once again be upright and looking over the right shoulder in the direction you will be traveling, allowing you to see where you will be skating and helping to keep your weight over the back of the right hip and the center back of your blade. Your toes should be slightly turned in and both knees bent. The majority of your weight should be on the left foot so that you can push from your left back inside edge onto a right backward outside edge.

Ensure that you do not lead with your backside. It should feel as if you were almost being pulled along by your right shoulder or side. Your free leg will be extended directly behind you over the tracing (heel to toe). Then you will slowly rise on the skating knee, again drawing the feet together so that they are parallel to each other. The right foot should be about half a foot farther back than the left due to the rotation of the hips, and both legs should be straight but not stiff. Then you will place the left foot onto the ice without pushing on an inside edge, lifting the right foot about an inch from the ice while keeping it parallel. After this you bend both knees before pushing from your back inside edge to the right outside edge again. This is repeated until your circle is completed.

You can then do the same on the other side but this time with the left hip and arm in the lead and traveling in a clockwise direction on a left back outside edge and a right back inside edge. Again, we would suggest that you count one, two and one in order to keep the movement fluid and rhythmic. It is very important for good skating that all movements be continuous and without stops in the knee action of the skating leg. You should be constantly rising or falling in all skating movements, so that your skating knee never reaches a total top or bottom position.

When you are confident on both sides, you should start to try this for the forward movement on a serpentine shape, again shifting your weight from one hip to the other as you draw your hip and foot through to change from one circle to the other. Make sure that you change your position from facing inside of one circle to facing inside of the other circle exactly in time with the rising knee. This will coordinate the whole movement and allow your head, arms, hips, and weight to change in an easy and natural way.

NB: That your weight remains up and over the right hip throughout this movement – head looks in the direction of travel and shoulders are facing the inside of the circle and parallel to the ice.

4. A basic right back outside edge as in Figure 1.

You should also find that you change direction from the top of your circle as you start to rise. When you change from one chassé to another you simply change from one circle to another, but you do not change direction. This exercise should allow you to skate in large bold half-circles joined together to form a serpentine shape. As you improve you will be able to cover at least half the width of the ice and, with increased speed, this will be fun to skate.

For the first time you should feel that now you can skate edges with some ease and have a nice continuous movement and feeling of changing your weight. Now would be the time to start to learn new skills like simple three turns, progressives, mohawks and choctaws. Take things in easy stages and have fun learning more interesting and complicated moves. Enjoy yourself and enjoy the wonderful art of figure skating. (The illustration shows a right backward chassé.)

3. Both knees bend strongly in preparation to push.

2. After the skating knee has risen you place the left foot onto an inside edge without pushing. Your weight should remain over the right hip.

1. A basic right back outside edge position with the right hip held back and your weight up and over the back of the right hip – arms and shoulder face inside of the circle, head held upright and looking in the line of travel.

Progressive Runs

Most beginners start by learning crossovers, as they are slightly easier, but the finished movement becomes a "progressive" step or movement. This movement is the power movement of every good skater, so time should be taken to achieve a good understanding of this step and some considerable time should be given to practicing this at every training session.

Forward Progressive Runs

This movement is sometimes incorrectly called "crossovers." If you start by learning a crossover, you would simply skate in a counterclockwise direction, crossing your right foot over the left, while keeping the left hip and arm forward as for the basic chassés. In the clockwise direction you should cross the left foot over the right, while maintaining the right side of your body forward. Again this exercise will make you skate in circles.

To develop this to "progressives" or "runs" you must push equally on both steps of the movement and, as the name suggests, the outside foot (the foot that crossed over previously) should now be placed ahead of the other by a foot or more in a progressive way. At the same time it is important to progress your body weight forward with the placing of the foot. Care should be taken to make sure that you do not put the foot forward without your body weight progression.

It is also normal that this movement is skated in what is called a "contra-body" position. This is where the hip and shoulder positions are held in opposition to one another. For instance, when the left hip is held forward to allow the hips to face slightly outside of the circle, the shoulders rotate to face inside of the circle, thereby bringing the right shoulder and arm forward, causing a twist and slight tension in the stomach, which is held in strongly.

On the first step the free leg should be turned strongly out, with thighs wide apart, and on the second step the free leg should turn naturally inward, causing the thighs to close together. This is a result of the hips facing outside of the circle and, as a result, the steps should always run to the outside of the circle. As always your hips and shoulders should remain parallel to the ice at all times. The free leg should be straight but not stiff while the skating knee rises and falls in a continuous way on each step.

Try to make sure that you are not down on the knee on the first step and up on the second. This is a common error with skaters, giving a very lopsided look, almost as if the skater had a wooden leg.

NB: This is usually skated in a contra-body position, that is, with the left hip forward and in the lead against the right shoulder and arm – see aerial diagrams.

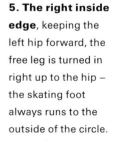

5. The right inside edge, keeping the left hip forward, the free leg is turned in right up to the hip – the skating foot always runs to the outside of the circle.

When you have the feeling for this rise and fall, this knee action can be changed from a direct rise and fall to a level but progressing movement. This feels as if your knees are converting the rising action into a forward movement or momentum, giving you the sensation of skating in a low-roofed corridor, so your skating knee stays active in the same way but pushes your body forward instead of being able simply to rise. (Here we show a left forward progressive run.)

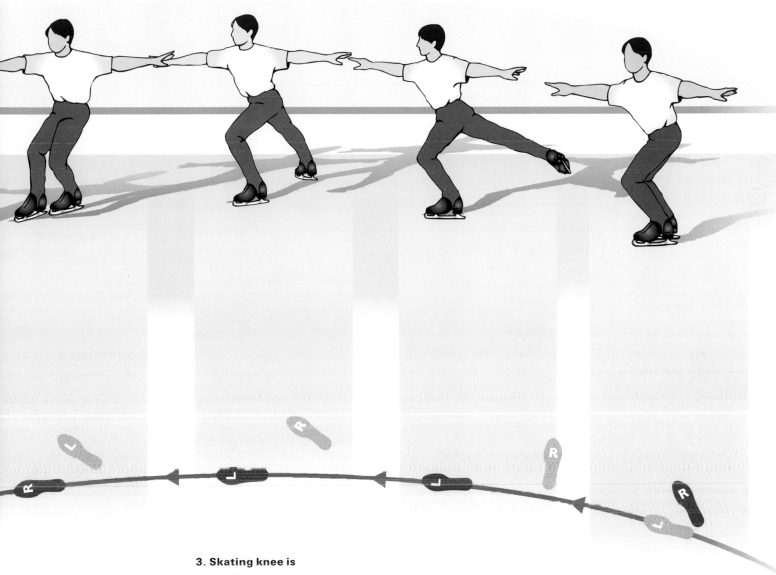

3. Skating knee is rising slightly and drawing the free leg through and forward.

4. This is **the progressive step** that gives the movement its name – note that the right foot is placed on the ice directly ahead of the left onto an inside progressive edge. It is important that the weight also progresses with the step.

2. Left outside edge with left hip leading against right shoulder on a strongly bent skating knee with the free leg extended and turned out.

1. Both knees are strongly bent with your weight on a right inside edge in preparation to push.

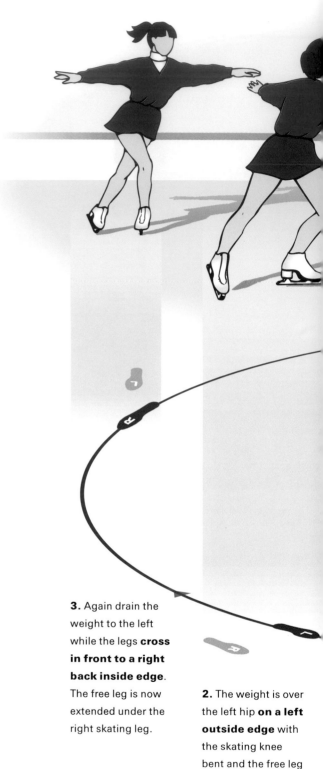

Backward Crossovers

This movement again will take you in a circle and is a way of building up to backward crosscuts and progressives, both of which are a little more difficult. Therefore it is best to practice this exercise first. There are two steps in this movement: first, when skated in a counterclockwise direction, a left back outside edge; second, a right back inside edge where you cross your foot over in front of your left foot. This is repeated while you skate your circle. It is important to face inside of your circle with your hips and shoulders, and to keep them parallel to the ice while maintaining your weight up over the back of your right hip throughout the steps. The skating knee action should appear to be continuous, bending, as always, both knees before pushing. You should be down in the knee during the right outside edge, rising to the cross in front of the left back inside edge. Your head should be up and over your right shoulder, looking in the direction that you are traveling. This is particularly important when skating backwards, so that you can see easily where you will be going, as this will allow you to feel more comfortable and at ease when traveling backwards, which at first can feel a little strange, as we do not normally walk backwards in our homes or the street!

This should then be skated in the opposite direction, keeping your left side back and again facing inside of the circle you are making. Make sure that you always develop both sides and directions equally, so that you do not have a bias for one side. It will become very important to be able to move in both directions with equal ease.

Backward Crosscuts

Backward crosscuts are the next development of a backward crossover. This step is nearly the same but skated with greater freedom and power with pushes on both steps. The basic position is exactly the same as for the crossover – that is, facing inside of the circle with hips and shoulders – but this time, having bent both knees, you thrust your weight diagonally back and into the circle, so that you step wide taking your body weight with you immediately over the new skating foot and onto an outside edge. At this point the legs are wide apart with the skating knee deeply bent and the free leg straight, still resting on the ice but without weight on it. You then thrust again up over the same hip and shoulder, thereby drawing your feet across each other.

Now you should find that you are on a back inside edge on the other foot, with your skating knee strongly bent and your free leg extended under you and turned in, with your thighs closed together. You then bring both feet back together and then bend both knees, keeping your weight

3. Again drain the weight to the left while the legs **cross in front to a right back inside edge**. The free leg is now extended under the right skating leg.

2. The weight is over the left hip **on a left outside edge** with the skating knee bent and the free leg straight but still lightly resting on the ice on an inside edge.

strongly on your inside edge, ready to thrust to the new skating foot to repeat the movement.

This should become a strong, powerful movement and is often used to gain power and speed in many skating movements and programs. Again this must be practiced in both directions, and always make sure that your head is up and looking in the direction you are traveling in, and that your shoulders and hips are parallel to the ice, with the arms extended naturally from the line of your shoulders.

This is one of the nicest movements both to perform and see. When you are confident, it really gives a sense of speed, almost like flying across the ice. (The illustration shows backward crosscuts to the left.)

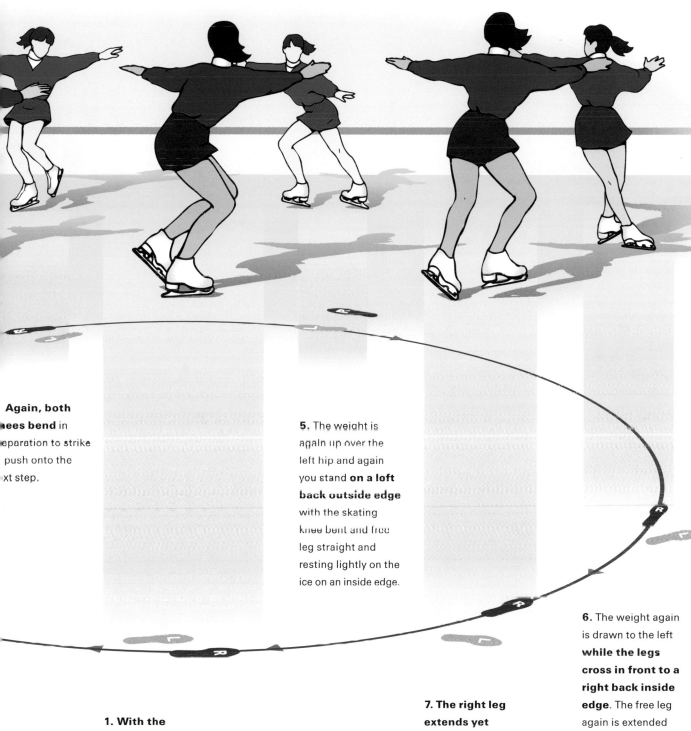

Again, both knees bend in preparation to strike push onto the next step.

5. The weight is again up over the left hip and again you stand **on a left back outside edge** with the skating knee bent and free leg straight and resting lightly on the ice on an inside edge.

1. With the weight on the right inside edge, both knees bend in preparation to push diagonally back and over the left hip.

6. The weight again is drawn to the left **while the legs cross in front to a right back inside edge.** The free leg again is extended under the right skating leg.

7. The right leg extends yet further on a right back inside edge.

NB: Throughout this movement the shoulders and hips face inside of the circle and the head is turned to the left to see where you are traveling. The weight should be over the back of the left hip.

Backward Progressive Runs

This movement, like the forward progressives, is similar to the crossover, but this time instead of crossing your foot in front you progress your new skating foot directly behind you by a distance of a foot or so. When skating in a counter-clockwise direction, you face inside of the circle with your right hip back and your weight up and over it. Bend both knees and push from your left inside edge onto a right back outside edge. Rise slowly on the right skating knee and at the same time draw the whole of the free leg past the skating foot and place the left foot onto the ice, heel first, directly behind you. This then becomes the new skating foot and your knees should be strongly bent and on a left back inside edge.

Again you should make sure that your weight progresses with your progressive step and do not let the foot go first and your body weight afterward. This is a major error. Again, the skating knee should rise as the feet return together to the basic position where the right foot will be about half a step behind the left foot. And then both knees bend ready to repeat the movement.

1. Both knees bend with the weight on the right back inside edge. **This position prepares you to push.**

ELVIS STOJKO, A TRUE ATHLETE.

2. Now on a basic left back outside edge with your weight over the back of your left hip and with your hips facing inside of the circle, the right leg is extended in front.

3. As the skating knee starts to rise the whole leg begins to be drawn in.

4. The right leg progresses directly behind the left. The weight should also be progressing at the same time in order to make the new and progressive step.

5. A right back outside edge being placed onto the ice directly behind the left foot. The hips then remain facing inside of the circle and the weight should remain over the left hip throughout this movement.

Cross Rolls

*These steps can only be skated on a serpentine shape
as they are performed from outside edge to outside edge
and, as their name suggests, the feet cross when placed
onto the ice. The word "roll" refers to the body action
as your weight rolls from one circle to another.*

Forward Cross Rolls

Your free leg should be extended forward of your body
during each step. This exercise should be practiced in both
directions. This step is used particularly in ice dancing.
(The illustration shows a left backward progressive run.)
The term "contra-body" should also be synonymous with
"cross rolls." This means that your upper and lower body
work in opposition to each other, so that when your right
hip is forward while skating on the right foot you would
have your left shoulder and arm forward against the hip.
Then, at exactly the time you rise to start to change to
the new foot, you should change shoulders and arms
rhythmically against your changing hip and foot. During
the skating of this movement your feet will both be turned
in, giving you a kind of pigeon-toed look and feeling, and
your feet should be slightly sickled to ensure that both are
constantly on outside edges.

   As you cross your feet to make your strike or push, your
weight should progress forward and diagonally, so that, as
you cross to the right foot, your weight moves forward to
the left side of your body. When you cross the left foot your
weight moves forward to the right side of your body. This
may seem illogical but you must remember that when you
are placing your right foot on the ice because your legs and
feet are crossed, your foot is now on the left side of your body.
With every step you should be driving onto a bent knee and
rising to draw your free leg through to the next step.
Throughout the movement your thighs should feel closed
and turned in and each step should form a full half-circle.
This should be skated to a rhythm one–two and one–two
and as you improve you can speed the movement up to a one
count. (The illustration shows a left forward cross roll.)

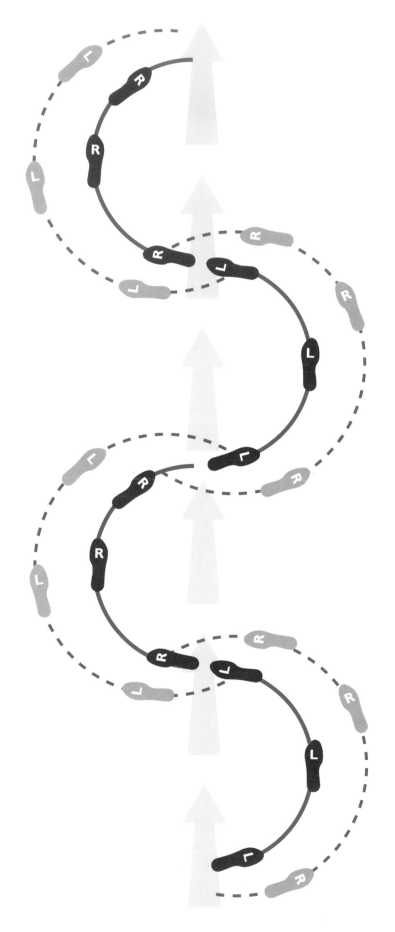

1. A left forward outside edge position skated in contra-body position – that is with the left hip forward against the right shoulder and arm. Skating knee is strongly bent.

2. The skating knee has risen and drawn the free leg in to cross in front. Both feet are turned in and the non-skating foot must be placed down and onto a right outside edge.

3. A right forward outside edge position skated in contra-body position. This movement should *always* be skated in contra-body position.

NB: This movement is usually skated in series as the step diagram shows and always on a serpentine shape, as each step makes a full half-circle.

3. A left back outside edge with the body facing outside of the circle.

2. As the skating knee rises the free leg is drawn in to cross behind – the legs are turned out throughout, the weight moves to the back of the left shoulder and the new skating foot is placed immediately onto a left back outside edge.

1. A basic right back outside edge position with the skating knee strongly bent.

NB: This movement is usually skated in series as the step diagram shows and always on a serpentine shape, as each step makes a full half-circle.

Backward Cross Rolls

Just as for forward cross rolls, this exercise is skated in a serpentine pattern due to the fact that each edge is an outside, but this time the feet cross behind rather than in front. Just as the feet were always turned *in* with forward cross rolls, here, your feet are permanently turned *out* at about 90 degrees.

Again, contra-body is the order of the day, with the hip movement against that of the upper body. It is very important that the body weight change behind you, and, as with forward cross rolls, the weight change is *across* your body, so that when you place your right foot down on the ice your weight changes to the back of your left shoulder and when you place the left foot onto the ice your weight moves to the back of your right shoulder. It is also important that you try to place the heel of your skating foot onto the ice first. Skaters often make the mistake of placing their toe picks onto the ice first, and this tends to make a noisy movement as well as slowing you down. It's also bad skating style.

As with forward, each step should start from a bent knee and rise during the transition to a new step and a bent knee. Speed should be gained not just by pushing but also by drawing the skate across the ice during the rising knee action, almost pulling the blade along as well as simply pushing. This is almost a hidden push and, as you improve your skating, you should use this method of movement more as it gives extra speed, flow, and ease of movement across the ice, helping to make it look effortless. An important attribute for the good skater! (The illustration shows a right back cross roll.)

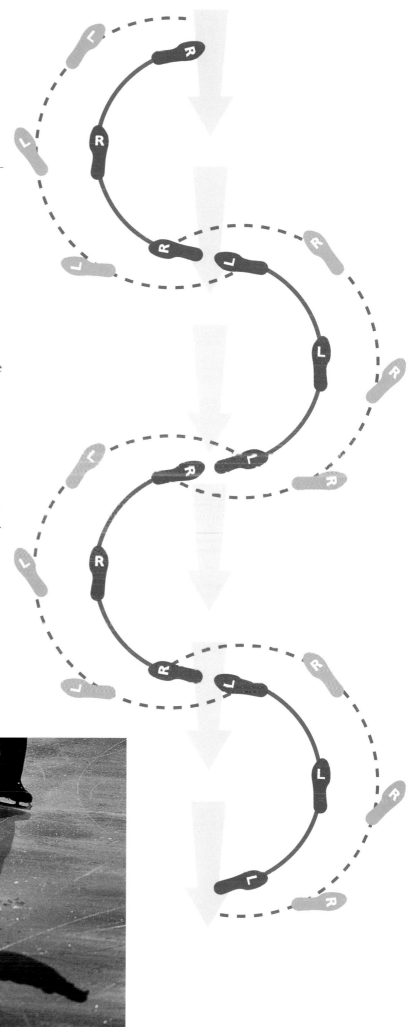

Three Turns

The name of this turn is taken from the shape that is formed on the ice when this turn is made (see illustrations). Each three turn is skated on one foot and on the four different edges: namely forward outside and inside turns and then backward inside and outside; then on the other foot, making a total of eight different turns in all. When learning all these turns we would suggest that you keep your head looking in the direction you are skating in, so that, as you prepare your turn, your head will appear to change from one shoulder to the other, but if you were looking at something you would not be aware of changing your eye line or view. This makes checking feel much easier as you become far less aware of turning.

The execution of each turn can be divided into five different sections, as we will find when dealing with jumps, which are: basic edge position; preparation; lift of the turn; check-out; and exit or runaway.

MIDORI ITO IN EXUBERANT MOOD.

ILLYA KULIK IN ELEGANT POSE.

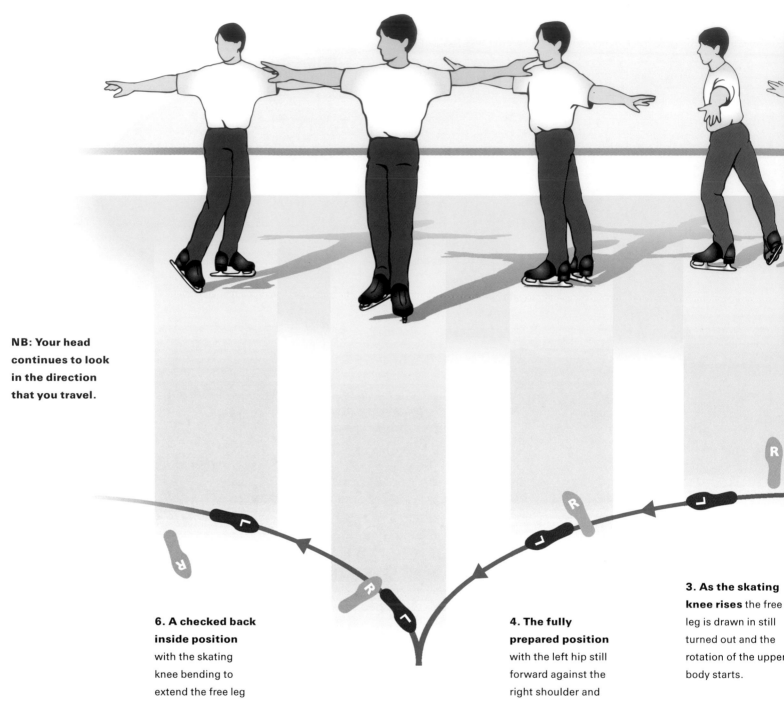

NB: Your head continues to look in the direction that you travel.

6. A checked back inside position with the skating knee bending to extend the free leg behind you.

5. The moment just after the turn when the skate has moved to a back inside edge and the upper body is "checking out" against the rotation of the turn.

4. The fully prepared position with the left hip still forward against the right shoulder and arm – the feet should be in a T position and the weight moves forward to the ball of the foot in readiness for the turn.

3. As the skating knee rises the free leg is drawn in still turned out and the rotation of the upper body starts.

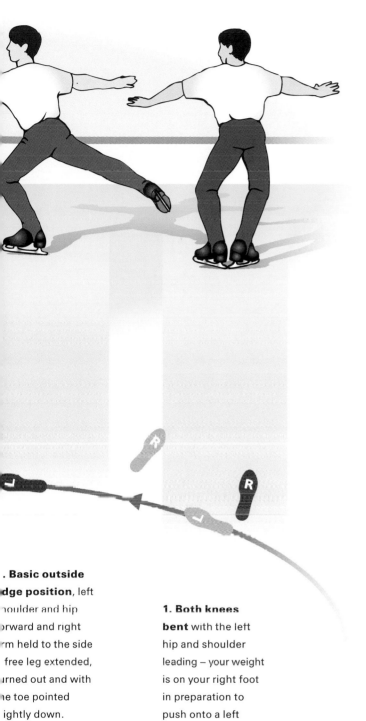

**. Basic outside
dge position**, left
houlder and hip
orward and right
rm held to the side
free leg extended,
urned out and with
he toe pointed
ightly down.

**1. Both knees
bent** with the left
hip and shoulder
leading – your weight
is on your right foot
in preparation to
push onto a left
outside edge.

The Forward Outside Three Turns

This is the most common turn and considered to be the
simplest. You should start by adopting your **basic position**
for an outside edge and we would suggest that you start
with the left foot, so your left hip and shoulder lead and face
approximately 45 degrees outside of the circle. The left arm
covers the proposed circle to be skated and the right arm is
held to the side. Your head should be held upright looking
forward and the feet in a T position with your weight on a
right inside edge.

You then bend both knees and push onto a left outside
edge, keeping the weight to the center back of your skate
and slightly into the circle. The free leg would be extended
directly behind you over the tracing.

The **preparation** starts as the skating knee begins to rise
and at the same time your upper body should rotate to face
inside of the circle and the free leg will be drawn in to touch
the skating foot in a 'I' position. Now, your right arm and
shoulder will be forward and over the proposed tracing
against the left hip, in what we could again describe as a
contra-body position.

At this point, just as your skating knee is nearly straight,
you should momentarily stop the rotation so that you can
lift the skating foot and the body weight over the ball of the
foot to a backward inside edge and **check-out** of the turn by
slightly reversing the shoulders and arms against the turn.
This now means that your right hip and shoulder would be
checked back and slightly down to help keep your weight on
the center back of your foot. Your body should be facing
inside of the circle with your body weight also slightly to the
inside of the circle to maintain a clean-running back inside
edge. The **exit** or **runaway**: as the skating knee bends the free
leg can extend away to make as beautiful a line as you wish.
This should then be repeated on the right foot and many
times until you are completely confident that you can achieve
this maneuver at speed and whatever tempo you wish, slow
or fast, and with total control and ease of movement.
(The illustration shows a left forward outside three turn.)

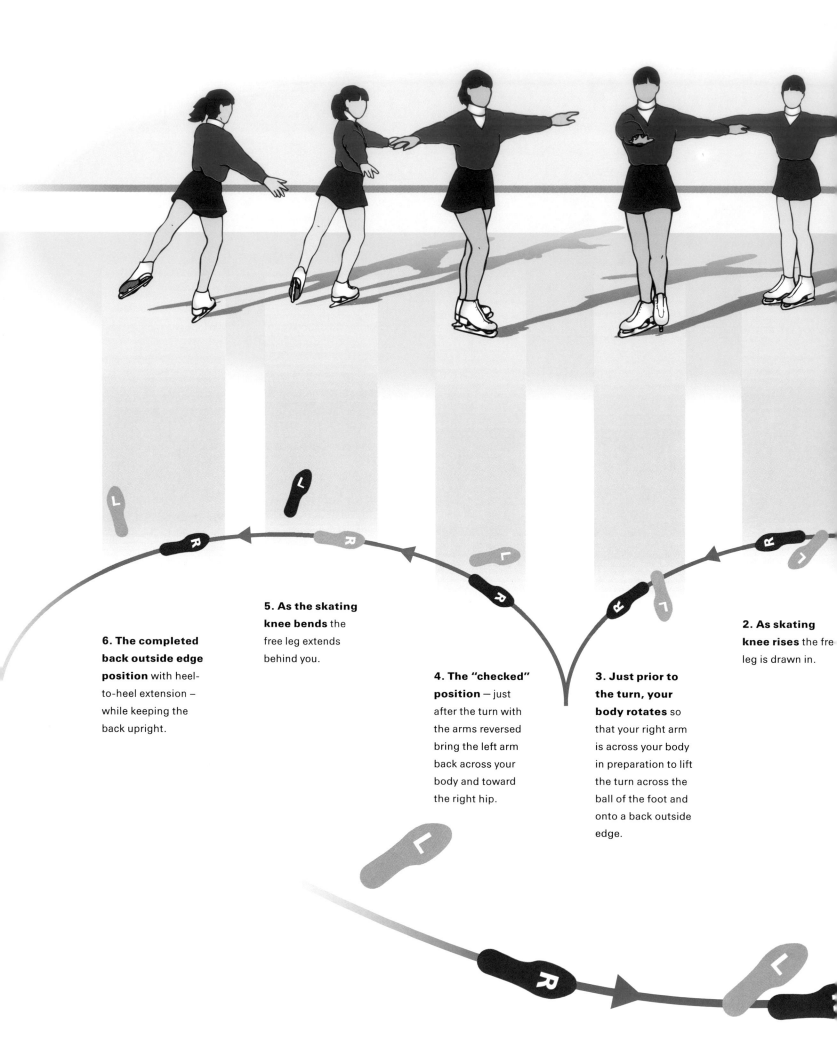

5. As the skating knee bends the free leg extends behind you.

6. The completed back outside edge position with heel-to-heel extension – while keeping the back upright.

4. The "checked" position — just after the turn with the arms reversed bring the left arm back across your body and toward the right hip.

3. Just prior to the turn, your body rotates so that your right arm is across your body in preparation to lift the turn across the ball of the foot and onto a back outside edge.

2. As skating knee rises the free leg is drawn in.

**Basic inside
edge position –
with left arm and hip
held forward – with
your free leg turned
out and toe pointed
slightly down.**

The Forward Inside Three Turns

These are the next steps to be mastered. Once again, start in a **basic position**. When starting on the right foot you should stand in a T position with the right foot in front and your weight on the back foot (left inside edge). The left arm, hip, and shoulder are forward and leading so that your body faces outside of the circle you plan to skate. You should bend both knees and push onto a right forward inside edge with your weight on the center back of your blades' radius. The **preparation** begins as the skating knee starts to rise and consists of a rotation toward the left so that your upper body now faces inside of your circle. At the same time the free leg is drawn slowly in to touch the skating foot.

The **lift of the turn** occurs just after your momentary stopping of your rotation, so that you lift your weight across the turn, over the ball of your foot to place the foot down again onto a right backward outside edge. At the same time you **check out** of the turn by slightly reversing your arms and shoulders, so that you finish with your right hip checked back and your right arm back along your tracing. Your left arm should now be across your body almost opposite your right hip. This means that your body is still facing inside of your circle.

The **exit** or **runaway** is as you bend your right knee still further to extend your free leg into a position behind you and over your tracing, with the leg turned out and toe pointed downward, leaving you free to choose what movement you would like to follow. At all times you should be in control and in a position where you choose what to do next. Never allow your lack of control to dictate what your next move will be! Again this should be repeated many times on both feet and at all speeds and tempos until this control is achieved. (The illustration shows a right forward inside three turn.)

The Backward Outside Three Turns

The backward turns for most skaters are considered to be a little more difficult but after a little practice they will soon become quite easy. The major difference is that, whereas the forward turn is executed over the ball of the foot, the backward turn is lifted from the back or heel of the foot/blade and it is often a help to think of lifting the foot to the outside of the circle, not to the inside, as this causes the weight to return to the toe of the blade. By this we mean that the blade itself covers an area to the outside of the circle during the moment of turn.

Once more you should start in your **basic position**, facing inside of the circle and if, for instance, you decide to perform a right back outside three, this would mean that your weight would be up over the back of your right hip, with your right arm over the tracing you intend to skate, and your left arm would be held inside of the circle nearly opposite your right hip (see illustration). Your weight should, as you start to push, change from your left inside edge to your right back outside edge.

Then, once more with the rising knee, the **preparation** begins. This time you will rotate outside of and toward the left side of your body, so that you will face to the outside of your circle, bringing your left arm back over the projected tracing and your right arm across your body and opposite your left hip. You should now feel that your weight has changed from your right hip to the back of your left hip. At this point you will momentarily stop your rotation to initiate the **lift** and **check-out**. You should **lift** your weight across the turn and over the heel and place the weight down onto a right forward inside edge. Again, during the **check-out**, you slightly reverse your upper body to keep it facing outside of the circle, and now you should find yourself with your left hip forward and your left arm across, opposite your right hip, and your right arm extended back behind you. Once more, as you bend your skating leg your free leg should extend forward over your tracing in an elegant manner. This would be your **exit** or **runaway**.

This should be repeated in both directions on both feet and once again at all speeds and tempos until you are confident of your own control and that you have no feeling of falling onto the other foot. Remember to practice with both feet and always bear in mind that all skating should look effortless and graceful at all times and that if possible you should never have an ugly line. If you do not feel one hundred percent confident and at ease, this will always show in your skating. Remember that good practice makes perfect! (The illustration shows a right back outside three turn.)

1. Basic back outside position – with hips and shoulders facing inside of the circle.

2. As the skating knee rises your hips and shoulders should rotate to face outside of the circle.

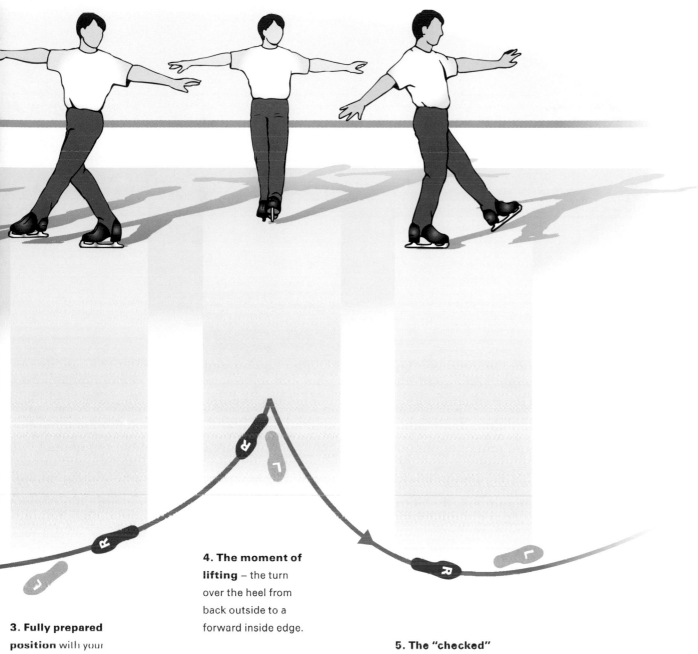

3. Fully prepared position with your weight on the heel of your skate.

4. The moment of lifting – the turn over the heel from back outside to a forward inside edge.

5. The "checked" position – keeping the left arm, shoulder and hip pressed forward – so that you still face outside the circle – skating knee is relaxed and slightly bent – free leg held forward in a toe-to-heel extension.

The Backward Inside Three Turns

This turn is the last in our family of threes, and soon you will be able to put these turns together in varying combinations to make interesting footwork and steps.

If you decide to skate a left back inside three you take a **basic position** from standing with the feet turned in and your weight on the right foot ready to push onto a left back inside edge. Having bent both knees first, thrust your weight back over the back of your left hip so that your shoulders and hips are facing outside of the circle with your right arm across your body and opposite your left hip. Your right arm should now be back over the tracing. As you rise on your skating knee you can slowly draw your feet closer together. This is the **preparation**.

Again you are now in a position to momentarily stop any rotation and **lift** your foot and weight over your heel onto a left forward outside edge. Once more, you should slightly reverse your upper body in order to **check-out** of the turn and in so doing you should subsequently find that you now have your left hip forward together with your left arm over your tracing. The right hip is held back and the right arm is checked to the side so that your body continues to face outside of the circle. Again the **exit** or **runaway** is achieved by bending the skating knee, hence getting a fully extended free leg and line.

As you improve at these movements you will find that you can make all kinds of interesting exercises for yourself including double threes, American threes and so on. You should always try to be adventurous and make your training and practice interesting and exciting by finding as many different ways of doing the same thing as possible. Never allow training to become a chore! (The illustration shows a right back inside three turn.)

NB: The body basically faces outside of the circle throughout this movement – head held upright and looking where you are going.

5. The skating knee now starts to rise toward the following movement.

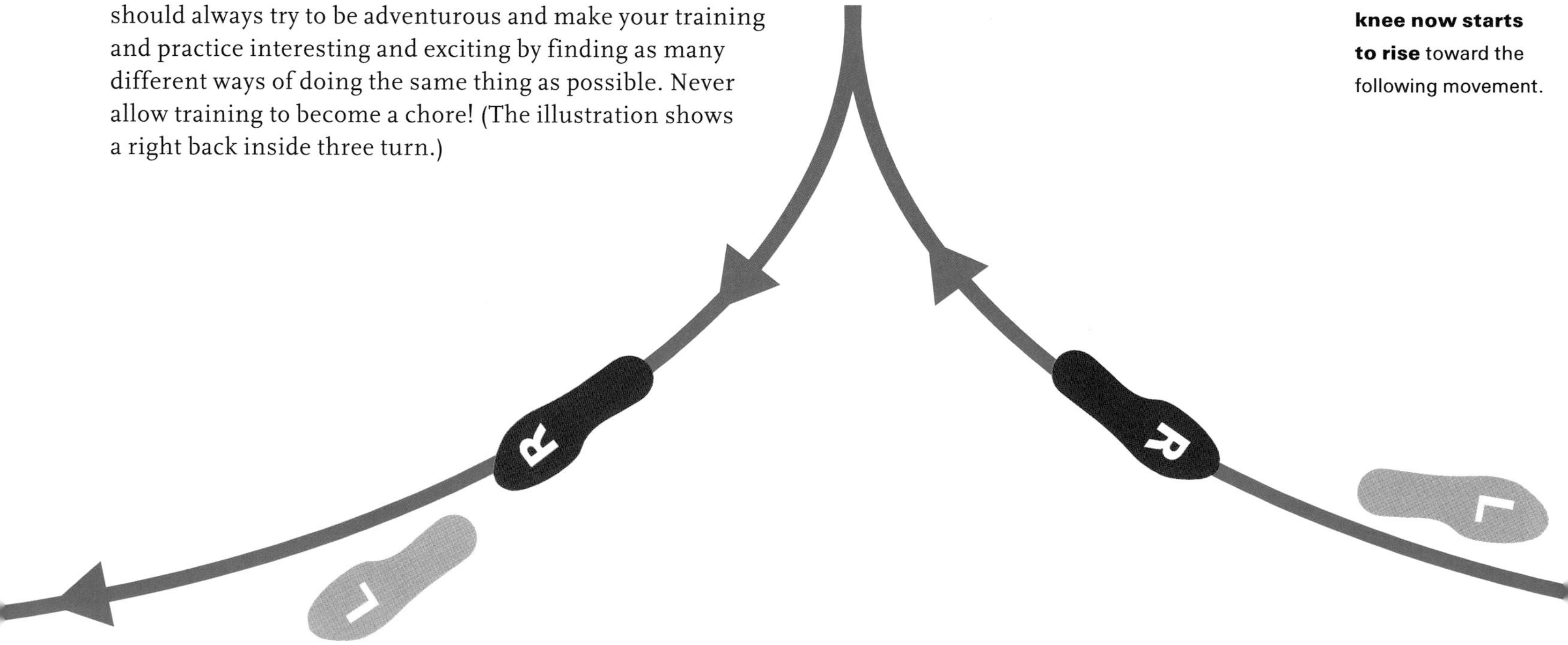

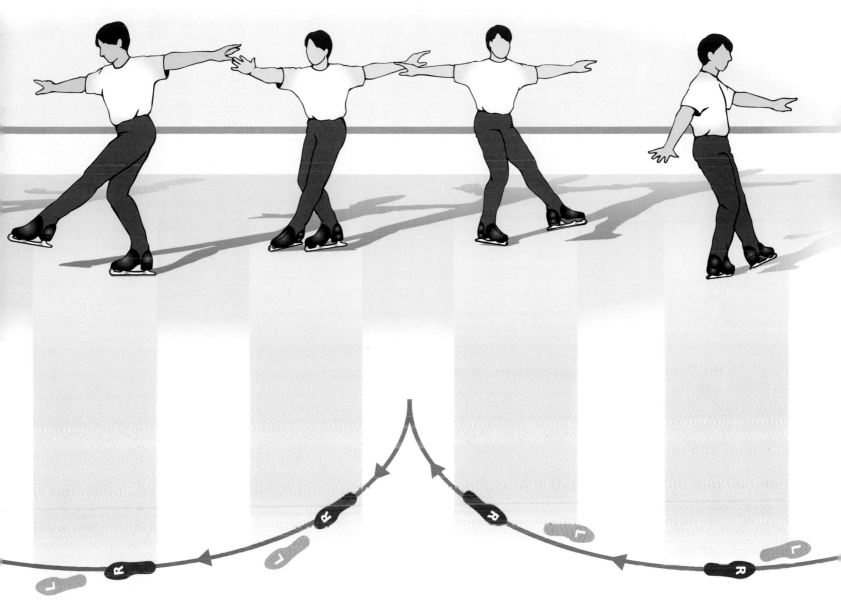

4. Basic outside edge position with the free leg extending forward while the skating knee continues to bend.

3. The checked position after the turn with the skating knee bent and the shoulders and hips parallel to the ice and keeping the right side leading.

2. The skating knee rising in preparation to lift the turn over the heel of the blade to a forward outside edge.

1. Basic back inside edge position with the weight over the back of your right hip – left arm held across your body, you are almost braced against the circle.

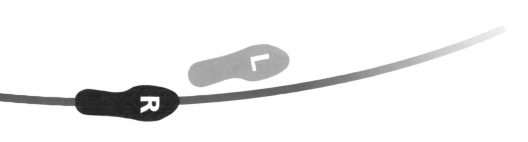

Mohawks

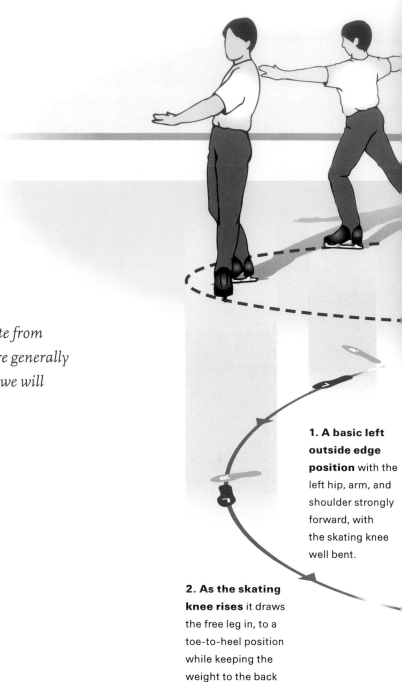

We now move on to the next major group of steps or turns. Some people refer to this step as a turn because you change direction from forward to backward, but this time you also change feet, unlike three turns. However, we prefer to think of a mohawk not as a turn but simply as a change of foot. This psychologically helps stop you seeing these steps as rotating.

Mohawks are always skated from either outside edge to outside edge or inside edge to inside edge. It is possible to skate from backward to forward but it is extremely unusual and they are generally seen only from forward to backward and it is only these that we will deal with in this book.

1. A basic left outside edge position with the left hip, arm, and shoulder strongly forward, with the skating knee well bent.

2. As the skating knee rises it draws the free leg in, to a toe-to-heel position while keeping the weight to the back of the left shoulder and hip. This is the preparation for the mohawk.

The Forward Outside Closed Mohawk

Let's start by describing a left forward outside closed mohawk, as this is usually the simplest one to start to learn and one of the most common. As usual you should start with a basic outside edge position, that is with your left hip and shoulder strongly forward with your left arm across your body so your hand is nearly opposite your right hip. Your right arm should be extended behind you over your tracing. Then, standing in a T position with your left foot in front of your right, you should bend both knees prior to pushing onto a strong left outside edge. After this, as you rise slowly on your skating knee, you once more draw your free leg in to place your toe to the heel of your skating foot. This should help pull your weight even more up over the back of your left hip and shoulder.

With your feet turned out at about 90 degrees you simply let your weight fall back toward your right heel until you can step onto a right back outside edge. You should find that your free leg extends forward automatically over the tracing of your right foot. Throughout the movement your hips and shoulders should remain parallel to the ice and as you change feet your new skating knee should bend softly to absorb your weight change. Just as with the three turn, you should check out of the mohawk by reversing your upper body and arms, so that now you should find yourself with your right arm across and in front of you, opposite your left hip, and your left arm extended in advance of your tracing.

Basically, your body has been facing outside of the circle throughout the movement (on both steps) and it is important to keep your weight in the circle throughout the mohawk.

We would also suggest that you keep your head looking over your left shoulder during this movement as it assists in stopping unwanted rotation.

As with all basic steps this should also be practiced on the right side and repeated many times to gain confidence and ease of performance. (The illustration shows a left forward outside closed mohawk.)

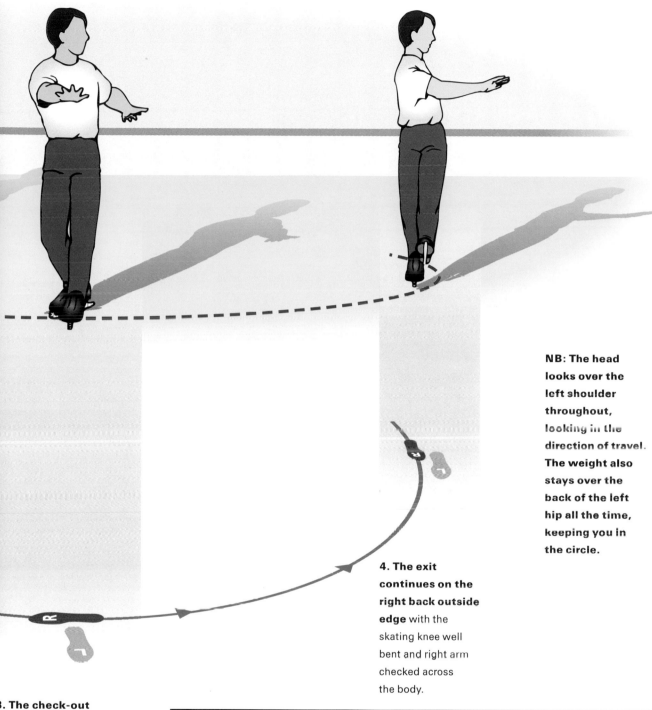

NB: The head looks over the left shoulder throughout, looking in the direction of travel. The weight also stays over the back of the left hip all the time, keeping you in the circle.

4. The exit continues on the right back outside edge with the skating knee well bent and right arm checked across the body.

3. The check-out is onto a right back outside edge, with the right arm checked across the front of your body and the weight still up and over the back of your left hip. The free leg extends in front over the tracing.

ALEXEI URMANOV
ACCEPTS THE APPLAUSE
OF THE CROWD.

The Forward Inside Closed Mohawk

This time we will try a left forward inside
mohawk, which starts from a basic inside
position. Your left foot is in front of the
right, which is placed in a T position. Your
right hip and shoulder are forward with your
right arm extended ahead of you and opposite
your left hip, and your left arm is held to the side
and outside of the circle. Next you bend both knees
and push from your right inside edge onto your left
inside with a strongly bent skating leg. Your weight should
be over your right hip. As you rise on the skating knee draw
your feet together into a toe-to-heel position and at the same
time your weight should slowly move toward the front of
your left hip.

Again, with your feet at 90 degrees to each other, you
should gently let your weight fall toward the heel of your
right foot, onto a backward inside edge. Your free leg
should automatically extend in front of your body and over
your tracing as your skating knee bends softly into a deep
movement. Also, at the same time as the new step takes
place, you again check your upper body against the
movement so that you continue to face inside of the circle
with your right arm now checked across your left hip and
your left arm now extended directly ahead of your line of
travel. It is a great help to keep your head looking over your
right shoulder throughout.

Once more this should be practiced on both feet and
until you are completely at ease with the movement at
speed and at varying tempos. Now start to include these
movements with all the others learned so far to make little
routines. Perhaps you can also start to introduce music of
varying styles and tempos to add greater interest and to
prepare you for the time when you can also add jumps and
other flourishes. Try not to be self-conscious and have a lot
of fun putting these movements and your ideas together.
(The illustration shows a left forward inside closed
mohawk.)

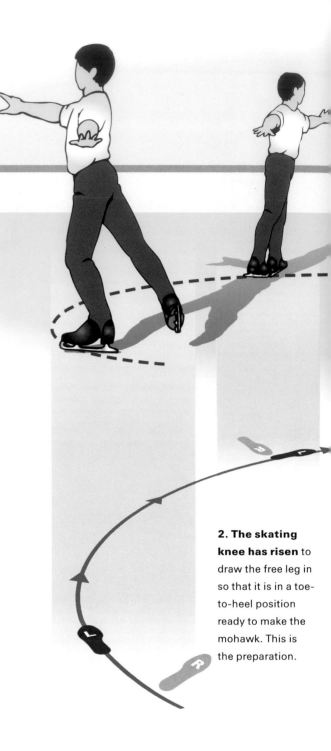

**2. The skating
knee has risen** to
draw the free leg in
so that it is in a toe-
to-heel position
ready to make the
mohawk. This is
the preparation.

**1. A basic left
forward inside
edge position**
with the right hip,
shoulders, and arm
leading – the skating
knee is strongly bent
and the free leg
turned out in a heel-
to-heel extension.

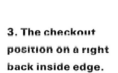

3. The checkout position on a right back inside edge. The skating knee is bending and the free leg is extended in front while the arms are checked with the right arm across the body opposite the left hip. The weight is up over the front of the left hip.

4. The exit position, as the skating knee continues to bend and extend the free leg to the maximum.

Paul Wylie entering a "pivot pose."

The Forward Inside Open Mohawk

Once again this is skated from forward inside edge to back inside edge but the big difference now is that, instead of placing your feet toe to heel, you place your feet heel to instep. The result of this is that your free leg will automatically want to extend behind you, instead of in front as with the closed mohawks. This gives the step its "open" tag because the hip position after the step is completely open whereas in the closed mohawks, where the free leg extends in front, the hip is considered closed.

In the right inside open mohawk you take the same stance as for the right closed mohawk, but as you rise on your skating knee you place your free foot to the instep of your right foot with both legs relaxed and flexed and at about 90 degrees to each other (T position). Also during the rising action your weight changes from your left hip over to the front of your right hip. Then you can simply step onto the heel of your left foot on an inside edge. By bending your new skating leg you can extend your free leg if you wish. As always, you should check out of this movement by reversing your body against the natural rotation. This means that you end with your left arm opposite your right hip and your right arm held ahead of the tracing. It is a help again to keep your head looking in the direction that you are skating in. In this case you should finish looking over your right shoulder. (The illustration shows a right forward inside open mohawk.)

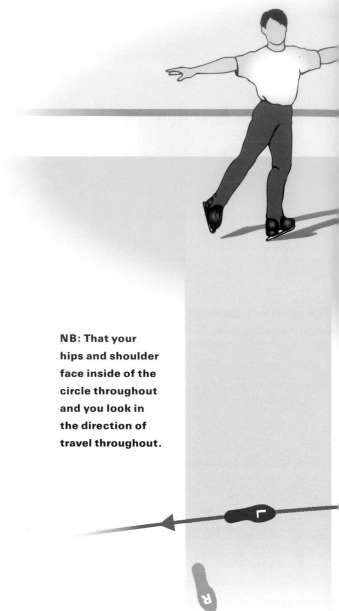

NB: That your hips and shoulder face inside of the circle throughout and you look in the direction of travel throughout.

TODD ELDRIDGE,
A TRUE STAR.

4. As the skating knee bends the free leg may be extended back over the tracing.

3. The left foot is placed onto a back inside edge, checking out to the right side of your body and keeping your weight onto the heel of this newly placed left foot. Make sure the skating knee is relaxed, not stiff.

2. As you rise on the skating knee the free leg is drawn in and the heel of the free foot is placed to the instep of the skating foot. At the same time the weight starts to move towards the front of the right shoulder in readiness for the mohawk.

1. A basic right forward inside edge position with the left hip held forward on a strongly bent knee.

1. A basic left outside edge position with the left hip, arm, or shoulder strongly in the lead. The skating knee should be bent and the free leg extended and turned out.

2. As the skating knee rises the free leg is drawn in to be placed with the heel to the instep of the skating foot. Care should be taken to ensure that you maintain an outside edge by keeping your weight over the back of your left shoulder.

3. The checked position on a right back outside with your weight still over the back of your left hip and shoulder. The skating knee is relaxed but not bent.

4. The exit position should be with the right arm checked across the body and keeping a right back outside edge. The free leg may then be extended by bending the skating knee.

The Forward Outside Open Mohawk

This step is skated from forward outside to back outside edge. If you wish to skate it on the left foot you will take up your basic left outside edge position with your left side leading. Then, as your skating knee rises, you draw your free foot in to place the heel along the instep of your skating foot, ensuring that your weight stays up over the back of your left hip. At this point you simply place the heel of your right foot down onto the ice on a right back outside edge and check out by reversing your upper body so that your right arm is now across your body opposite your left hip and your left arm is held to the side.

Your weight should stay over the back of your left shoulder and hip and again we suggest you keep your head looking over your left shoulder throughout, then train the other side in the same way. (The illustration shows a left forward outside open mohawk.)

TODD ELDRIDGE IN
EXHIBITION.

Choctaws

A choctaw varies from a mohawk in that this movement will be skated to opposing edges. That is to say inside to outside or outside to inside. In doing this the movement will change from one bold half-circle to another, whereas the mohawk continues on the same circle.

The Forward Inside Closed Choctaw

For the left forward inside closed choctaw you start once more in your basic inside edge position, with your right hip and shoulder leading and your right arm opposite your left hip with your left arm extended to the side. Next you bend both knees before pushing onto your left inside edge and your weight should be firmly up over your right hip. Then, as you rise on your skating knee, you draw your feet together once more in the toe-to-heel position and at the same time your weight should gradually transfer diagonally across your body toward the back of your left shoulder and hip, in preparation for the new step. This should happen without your changing edge.

    Then, with your feet in an L position, let your weight gradually fall toward the heel of your right foot and onto an outside edge. At the same time strongly check out and allow the skating knee to bend deeply. You now find that your free leg is extended forward over the right tracing foot, your right arm should be checked across your body opposite your left hip, and your left arm should be extended to the side and slightly back to help keep your weight up and over the back of your left hip. This helps to keep you on a strong back outside edge but this time facing outside of the new circle. Put simply, you could say that you face outside of both circles as much as possible. Again this should be repeated on both feet until you are happy with the way you can do this. Make sure that you keep this movement rhythmical, so your weight changes easily and with fluidity. (The illustration shows a left forward inside closed choctaw.)

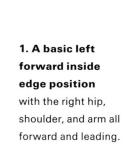

1. A basic left forward inside edge position with the right hip, shoulder, and arm all forward and leading.

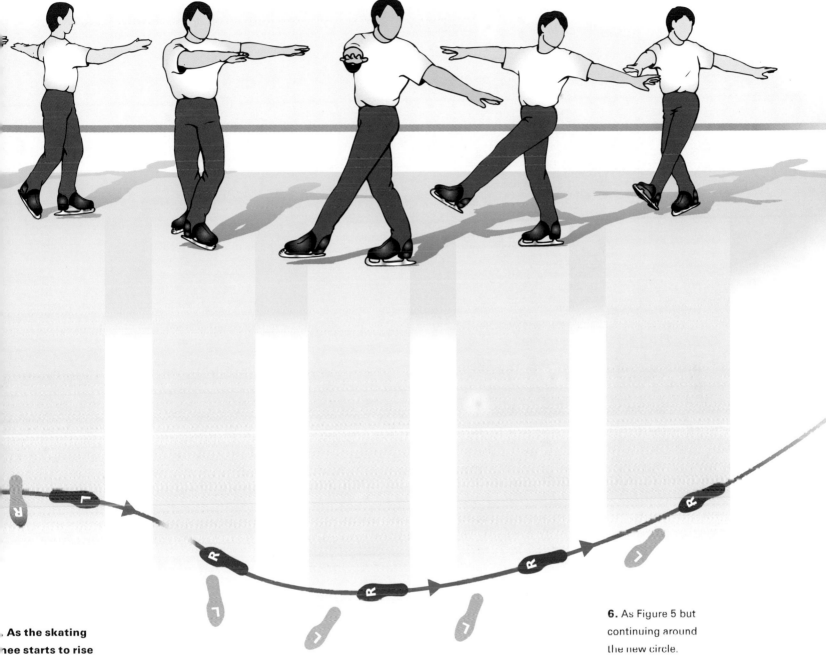

. As the skating nee starts to rise e free leg is drawn and starts to cross e tracing of the ating foot, and ur weight should art to change agonally towards e back of your left houlder. Note that e right arm stays rward in a countertated position.

3. The turn or step takes place from a toe-to-heel position, and from a left forward inside to a right back outside edge.

4. The checked-back outside edge position with the right arm checked across your body and your weight to the back of your left shoulder, with the skating knee bending.

5. The exit position is a strong outside edge with the free leg held in front with the heel of the free foot over the toe of the tracing foot.

6. As Figure 5 but continuing around the new circle.

NB: The movement will always take you from one circle to another as the choctaw is performed – choctaws are always to opposing edges.

KATARINA WITT IN
ARABESQUE POSE.

The Forward Outside Closed Choctaw

For the left outside closed choctaw you should start in your basic outside position, that is with your left side strongly forward, left arm forward, and right arm held to the side. With your feet in a T position with the left foot in front and both knees well bent, you then push onto a strong left outside edge. As your skating knee rises you draw your feet together into another toe-to-heel position, ensuring that your weight stays strongly up and over the back of your left hip. Then you let your weight fall across your back to the heel of your right foot and onto a back inside edge. At the same time your new skating knee bends deeply and you check your arms across you, so that your right arm is now opposite your left hip and your left arm is held to the side and over the proposed tracing line.

Your free leg should once again be extended forward from your body and over the tracing of your right inside edge, so that the heel of your free leg is directly on or slightly across the tracing, while keeping your thighs closely together. Repeat this movement on both feet until you can skate it with ease.

Forward and Backward Open Choctaws

These can be skated consecutively from forward inside edge to back outside edge and, if you are good enough, back again to forward inside edge, creating the second and backward choctaw. This is a difficult step because it is not possible to give a direct push, but instead you have to work the edges themselves to gain speed, getting what is called a "hidden push" from your resistance from your knee bend and pressure against the ice. However, when you have achieved this you are really starting to come to terms with the skills of figure skating.

Start with a left forward inside edge, keeping your right hip forward and your right arm while looking strongly over your left shoulder. Your right free leg should be extended forward. As you rise slightly on your skating knee you should flex your free foot so that you can place it heel to toe onto a back outside edge. Keeping your weight over the back of your left hip, you then bend your new skating knee very strongly, while your free leg is held open and back into the circle. You put your left foot back, toe to heel, onto a forward inside edge, once more on a deep edge and with a deep knee-bend. During this movement your arms should check rhythmically against your hips, keeping the knee action and arms working in contra-body throughout. This should then be repeated on the other side.

Brackets, Counters, and Rockers

These are the final turns to be learned and, like three turns, are turned on the same foot. However, we will not be covering these in detail but will simply say that the **rocker** is a turn, like a **three turn**, rotated into the circle but, because you turn to the same edge as you are already skating on, you move off into a new circle (see diagram). The **bracket** is the reverse of the three turn, because it turns or rotates against the circle. The **counter** is like a bracket rotated against the circle but turned from and onto the same edge, which causes you again to skate into a new circle (see diagrams).

This now gives you all the major groups of steps so you can now enjoy putting them together in unusual combinations. And remember that the world is now your oyster. Your originality and your skating ability are all that stand between you and the skating greats. You should also try to coordinate different arm movements and styles into your training – learning to use your whole body to help create the pictures and emotions that help make figure skating such a stunning and scintillating sport-cum-art form.

A DRAMATIC "SKID STOP."

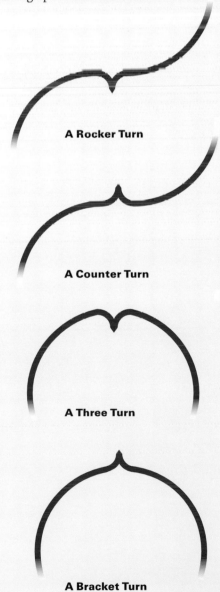

A Rocker Turn

A Counter Turn

A Three Turn

A Bracket Turn

Children's Fun Skating

Having fun when learning should always be of great importance and this is particularly true when dealing with a leisure sport and young people. Training and learning become much easier when variety and fun aspects are included in your schedule and to this end we are including a short section on games and ways of using them to improve your skating.

It is usually more pleasurable and more productive to learn in a group because you gain a "group energy," which makes hard work easier and less tiring, especially on the bad days, as well as developing a more competitive atmosphere.

A simple game of "Tag" (or " It ") can, for instance, be fun for all while you learn a lot about basic skating skills and agility. Tag is playable by as many people as you want, from two to 50 or more. Safety should be an important factor, so young people should be supervised at all times, as in all training group activities. One person in, say, ten is nominated as " It " or "lead person," perhaps wearing a baseball hat or something that all the other players can recognize easily from a distance, then " It " players try to catch and touch (tag) as many of the other players as possible.

When caught, the tagged players have to stand still and shout "Help" as loudly as possible, and they then can be rescued by two or more of the other players, holding hands and circling the captive stationary player twice. They are then free and able to continue in the game. This is great fun with skaters of all ages and helps develop stamina, agility, edge control, speed, and maneuverability, plus a feeling of team spirit and group bonding.

What more could you want from such a simple game?

Other games to be recommended are "Go–Stop," which is just skating forward and stopping when the leader shouts stop. This is good for beginners to learn to stop quickly and then can be developed to include turning or spinning, jumping, or whatever the leader calls.

Whole-body movement and a growth in choreographic skills can also be developed by getting a group of skaters to skate down the center of the rink in twos concentrating on moving a certain part of their body as much as possible. For instance, arms, head, pelvis, wrist, back, or legs – it doesn't matter which because the skater will become more and more aware of how to "isolate" their movements and feel how their body works, not only in each area but as a whole.

The skaters then return along the side of the rink to where they started to receive the next command.

It's also a good idea to always finish by trying to move the whole body and you will be amazed how quickly you learn to move yourself in a free way. This should also be done to varying styles of music to add even more interest and fun.

Remember that even when working on your own and skating at whatever level you are at, beginner or competition skater, training and training sessions should be fun and as varied as possible. Never let skating become boring. Always vary what you do and always have fun practicing while trying to improve. Variety is the spice of life and skating is great fun. Enjoy what you do. Feel the wind in your hair and have a smile on your face.

Free Skating

Free skating is perhaps the most popular of all the skating forms. Free skating around the world has an enormous participation level with skaters of all ages attempting to jump and spin, spiral and spread-eagle, with or without music. Free skating is very much an individual sport with participants working on their own with only the assistance of a coach for both technical and moral support.

Free skating at competition and championship level must follow strict and well-defined rules which have been set down by the ISU. The ISU administer the sport and make the rules for all national and international events. Free-skating events comprise two sections. The first is a "short" program followed by a "long" free-skating program. The short program contains a fixed number of elements, which must not be repeated. The elements will be the same for all skaters and the length of the program should be no longer than 2 minutes 40 seconds.

In every event the short program is very important and can be the most nerve-racking. The long free-skating program varies in length according to the category, but at championship level can range from 3 minutes to 4 minutes 30 seconds. The length of the program is different for men and women, with men always skating a longer program, for example, 4 minutes for women and 4 minutes 30 seconds for men at senior level.

Within the long free-skating program the skater must skate certain elements, but in general the skater has free choice to include whatever they can do.

Today's free skaters at championship level will include all of the triple jumps as well as quadruple jumps. Triple jumps are integrated to make complex combination jumps. Spins range from single-position spins to combined-position spins and very athletic jump spins. Footwork is very complex with obligatory step sequences containing steps that sometimes appear to be impossible.

Artistry is also a very important area and today's skaters spend hours working on the presentation of their program to gain maximum marks from the judges.

Costume plays a very important role for the competitive skater. Many skaters today do not simply skate to a piece of music but they will interpret a story, and the costume and the choreography must therefore illustrate the theme of the program. The choice of costume and music is most important – often the wrong music and costume will be selected for a skater and the judges will make a deduction in their marks. Great care should be taken over choice of music as it should suit the age and ability of the skater.

Free skating has moved on so very quickly in recent years that one can only wonder at what the future holds. Skaters from around the world are getting very much stronger as the years go by with one generation of skaters

FLIGHT AND ROTATION POSITION.

demonstrating more difficult jumps and spins than the generation before. Skaters are also getting younger. Being World Champion at 15 is no longer a dream but a reality.

As with all sports, good groundwork is really the most important factor for acquiring a really good, solid technique. Figure skating is a very long, slow process: you must be very patient and not expect too much too soon. However, with good guidance and patience you can accomplish a lot in free skating.

The following pages are intended to give you sound guidelines to help you improve on your current technique or give you an awareness of the demands before you embark on what is the wonderful world of free skating.

JUMPS
GENERAL PRINCIPLES

Jumping on ice for most skaters is the most exciting part of ice skating. The thrill of jumping, turning in the air, and landing safely on the ice adds a special dimension to figure skating. Safety when jumping is of paramount importance and no jump should be undertaken without first having learned thoroughly the basics of figure skating. Jumps should be attempted only under the watchful eye of a qualified coach to avoid any danger of learning incorrectly.

AN EXCELLENT LANDING POSITION.

There are five rules or principles that all jumps must adhere to and they should be followed carefully. They are:

1   The Preparation.
2   The Take-off,
3   The Flight and Rotation.
4   The Landing
5   The Exit.

Let's look at each section separately.

The Preparation

This section, like all sections of a jump, is very important. It is the section before the take-off in which you must prepare yourself for the jump. Today's very advanced skaters will prepare for their jumps with a great deal of speed and in many cases with complicated footwork and step sequences. For the beginner the preparation should consist of strong edges and good simple positions. Each jump needs a different preparation but on each one you must ensure that your back is upright, your head held high, and arms are extended, and be very positive about what you are about to do. If your preparation is weak, the jump will be too.

The Take-off

The take-off is the point where you actually leave the ice. Each jump has a different take-off. Some are from forward, others from backward. Jumps have different take-off edges, too, outside or inside, according to the jump. Timing the take-off is very important. You will, for the first time, really use your toe pick or toe rake. The take-off must be very well controlled. Your body, arms, legs and head must all be under control and work together to achieve a strong take-off. A good take-off will ensure a safe jump, because most of your problems with a jump could stem from it.

The Flight and Rotation

This section of the jump is when you have taken off and are in the air. Jumps range from half a turn, through to four rotations in the air. The more rotations required, the faster you must rotate. The rotating position in the air is very similar for all jumps but changes in power according to the number of rotations being attempted. Trying to defy gravity by staying in the air for the longest time will help give you more time to rotate. Try for a very tall position during the jump with your head held high, the body upright, hips forward, and, according to the jump, your arms and free leg held close to the body (see photograph). All rotation must be stopped in the air before landing or the jump will be "over-rotated." You might even fall over.

The Landing

All jumps, regardless of difficulty, will have a similar landing. The landing should be strong, but also very smooth and light. All landings are on the backward outside edge of the blade and, of course, the landing must be clearly and cleanly executed on one foot. Touching down with the free foot is a big mistake. Avoiding a fall on the landing is also very important. A good take-off and jump will help to ensure a good landing.

The Exit

This is the final section. It should be held on the outside edge for as long as possible to demonstrate control. The body position on the exit is very important. Should you wish to combine two jumps, a strong exit and landing will make the second jump a lot easier to do. A jump can be made to look even better by holding different arm and free leg positions on landing. This should be done only when you have mastered the jump.

4. The landing and the exit positions.

3. Flight and rotation position in the air.

2. Forward outside edge take-off.

1. Backward outside preparation edge.

SURYA BONALY
DEMONSTATES A
SPLIT JUMP.

The Three (or Waltz) Jump

This is where your real jumping days start! Probably the easiest of jumps but without doubt the most important. The waltz jump is the bedrock for the Axel, double Axel, and the famous triple Axel.

Before learning this jump, you must find out which leg you most naturally jump from. The majority of skaters jump naturally from left to right but there are lots of skaters who also jump from right to left. Your coach will soon tell you which way is better for you, but try both directions, and you'll soon find out which you prefer.

The waltz jump contains one half of a full rotation in the air, jumping from forward to backward. The take-off is from a forward outside edge with the landing on the backward outside edge of the opposite foot.

The preparation can be done in many ways. The easiest is by skating several backward crosscuts on a circle to gain speed, then standing on a backward outside edge on the same circle facing out of the circle, with the free leg well extended behind you, your head looking where you are going and your arms well extended (see diagram).

You must then close your feet, bend both knees, and step from backward to forward onto a forward outside edge. Your new skating leg must bend very strongly and your skating hip and shoulder should lead, with the free side of the body slightly pressed back. Both arms should be slightly behind the body (see diagram).

You are now ready to take off. From your already strongly bent skating knee start to push up from the knee and ankle. Your arms should move forward together with the free leg. Your body weight will move forward along the blade and just prior to take off you should feel yourself going over the toe rake of the blade as you lift strongly into the air. As you lift up, both arms and free leg move quickly forward to the front of the body (think of reaching forward to take hold of a pole). The arms should make a small arc to the front of the body, no higher than the shoulders. Your head should be high with your eyes looking up (towards the "pole"), and both legs nicely extended, creating an arc. This is known as the "top of the jump." You must be very strong at this point or your jump might give way (see diagram).

As your body weight moves forward it should transfer onto the free leg. Both arms must open, to stop the rotation, in readiness for the landing. On landing, the toe rake of the new skating foot touches the ice first (avoid landing on the full blade), followed immediately by the backward outside edge. The skating leg should bend strongly to absorb the body weight. The free leg moves quickly behind, and should be held high and extended with the free foot nicely turned out. Both arms should be well extended, with the free arm slightly in front of the body. Ensure that your head, as always, is held high and your shoulders are kept down to avoid any hunching (see diagram).

The exit position (see diagram) is common to all jumps. This position can, at a later stage, be varied to make the exit position look more attractive, particularly when skating to music, as you, with your coach, can adapt the positions to suit the music.

The Axel

The Axel is classed as the first of the double jumps. It has one-and-a-half revolutions in the air, has a forward take-off and lands backwards on an outside edge. This jump should be attempted only when all of the single jumps have been mastered and are under control. It would be foolish to rush the Axel as it is a most important jump and mistakes learned early on will be very difficult to correct at a later stage. The Axel is a combination of two other jumps: the waltz and the loop. The waltz jump has half a revolution and the loop jump (see page 86) has one revolution. When learning the Axel, practicing the waltz and loop jumps together is a very good exercise. Remember that, when you combine the two jumps, the free leg, after the waltz jump, should be left in front and you may then jump immediately into the loop jump.

One other preparation is the backward outside upright spin (see Spins). This spin gives you the feel for rotating very quickly in a perfect position, which would be the true position for all double, triple and quadruple jumps. Both the jump combination and the backward outside upright spin should be mastered before you attack the Axel.

6. The exit position, strongly held on a backward outside edge.

5. Prior to **the landing**, with the free leg forward.

The Single Axel

The Axel starts rather like a waltz jump: the preparation is the same, as is the take-off. The big difference is that more knee-bend will be required to give the jump more height, thereby giving you more time to rotate in the air. The take-off is from a forward outside edge. It must be a very clean take-off from the toe rake without any skidding or turning before you execute the maneuver. To avoid turning before take-off, ensure that the left side of your body is firmly pressed forward to stop the skating side from rotating. On

take-off, the free leg and both arms are brought forward together at the same time as you push up and into the air. As the first half-turn is taking place, you must then quickly "snap" both arms in toward the body and allow the free leg to remain in front (see rotational diagram). If the take-off is well executed you will find the free leg will naturally position itself correctly to the front.

The head should be held high, looking in the direction of the jump, never downward. Once you have snapped your

Notice that the ee leg during e rotation is not o crossed. Arms se to the body t not too tight.

3. Thrusting forward and **up over the toe**, using both arms and your free leg.

2. Strongly bent take-off leg. The head should be held high.

1. Backward outside edge – make sure you have well-controlled shoulders and hips.

arms toward your body, the speed of rotation will increase and the remainder of the rotation will be made. This sounds easy but is very difficult and will require lots of practice. Almost as soon as the arms have been snapped in they must then be opened again before landing.

The timing of the arm pull is very important and is possibly the most important aspect of any double or triple jump. The pull will create and control the rotation: the harder the pull, the more rotation; the less pull, the slower the

rotation. Often only one arm will pull in and you will find that the other will fly away, or maybe you will not pull in at all, creating all sorts of problems. Lots of time should be spent off ice practicing pulling the arms in and out very quickly to develop a good "snap" technique. Doing this combined with off-ice jumping is a very good way to develop jumping technique.

The landing for the Axel is the same as for all jumps and the landing should be held for as long as possible.

7. A very strong exit position, with the head held high.

6. Open both arms and **uncross your free leg** before landing.

5. At the **top of the jump,** feet crossed and arms tight to the body.

4. Starting the **rotation.** Both feet are off the ice.

3. Leave the ice cleanly over the toe rake; avoid skidding or turning on the ice.

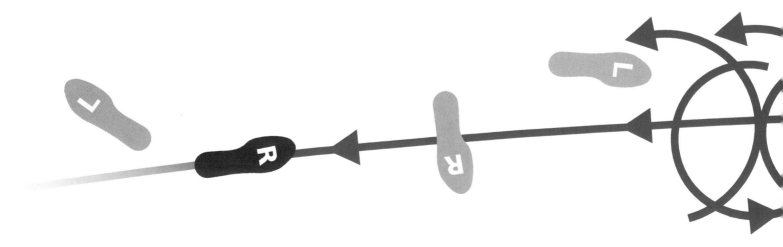

The Double Axel

Although classed as a double jump, the double Axel is really a part of the "triple" family of jumps. The double Axel has two-and-a-half revolutions in the air. The take-off and landing are practically the same as for the single Axel, the big difference being the extra rotation in the air.

The key to the double Axel and all triple jumps is the speed at which you rotate and the speed at which you can effectively get into the spinning position in the air. The spinning position of the double Axel is that of a double loop (see page 88), and this position will be the same for all triple jumps (i.e. the single plus a double loop). Therefore the double Axel is a waltz jump followed in the air by the double loop. The only way that this can be achieved is by mastering the pulling in and out, the "snap" technique we saw earlier. The take-off is of course very important and even more knee-bend will be required on the double Axel than on the single to try to gain even more height.

Height will give you time in the air, and although very little time is spent in the air it is crucial to have as much as possible in order to complete the two-and-a-half revolutions. The diagrams show the various stages of the jump.

The only real way to achieve the double Axel is to have an excellent basic jumping technique. It is for this reason that spending lots of time on the basic foundations of skating technique is so important.

As for the single
el, always ensure
t the **left side**
 the body
 forward.

1. The preparation must be well planned.

GRACE AND DRAMA COMBINED IN ONE POSITION.

The Triple Axel

The triple Axel has three-and-a-half rotations in the air. It is almost a quadruple jump and is very, very difficult.

Once again the basic principles are the same as for the waltz jump, Axel and double Axel, but now the speed of rotation is absolutely critical.

The triple Axel should be skated very quickly and in most cases is not only very high with fast rotation but also very long. The entry speed should be converted into height and length allowing you the extra time to rotate in the air.

In today's very competitive skating world the triple Axel is even combined with the triple toe loop or the triple loop. This makes it a very impressive jump, and it's vital for male skaters should they wish to compete at World and Olympic Championships. Follow the diagrams for a better understanding of the triple Axel.

A GOOD ROTATIONAL POSITION.

7. The landing will be on a very strong, deep, backward outside edge.

6. Open the arms very strongly to stop the three-and-a-half rotations.

5. The very stron and sharp snap the arms to give **rotation**.

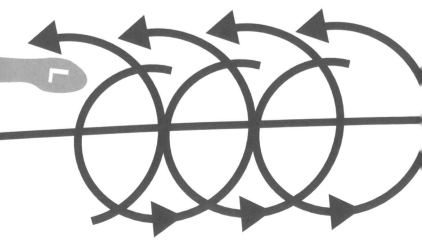

4. The first phase is delayed while **gaining height**.

3. Jump as high as possible in the direction of the outside of the curve.

2. Enormous power, rhythm and timing required on this **take-off**.

1. Begin in same way as for double.

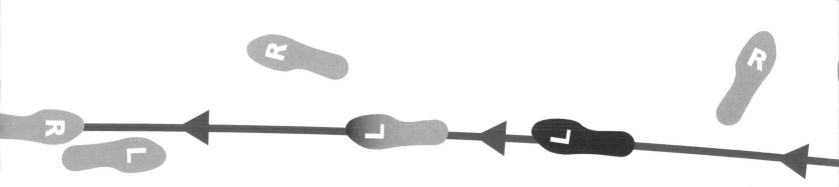

The Salchow

After the waltz jump (see page 67) the next one to learn is the Salchow – named after Ulrich Salchow, a Swedish and World Champion. The Salchow can be developed, as can all jumps, into the double, triple, and even the quadruple Salchow.

Now that you know which leg you jump from and in which direction you rotate, the Salchow will be a little easier to learn.

6. The landing and exit positions.

5. The flight position.
Not too tight.

The Single Salchow

The single Salchow, unlike the waltz jump, has a backward take-off and from an inside edge. The preparation stage is very similar to that of the waltz jump, with a backward outside edge following several crosscuts on a circle. You must then step from backward to forward, stepping outside of the circle and onto an outside edge with your skating side leading (see diagram).

At this point you must do a three turn, taking you from forward outside to backward inside. This three turn should be skated as you've already seen, but it is much larger and deeper, with the free leg very well extended behind you before and after the three turn. Once the three turn has been done, you will be on a backward inside edge, your free leg and arm extended behind with the left arm in front. You should be looking to the front, and the skating knee should be very well bent. At this point you are ready to take-off.

You should practice the three turn position, without jumping, until you have mastered the necessary control of the shoulders and hips, as "swinging" this section of the jump is very common.

When you feel comfortable with the three turn, the take-off should be attempted. To take-off, the skating knee should bend a little more. This will make the backward inside edge deepen (leaving a hook-like tracing on the ice). The free arm and free leg should be brought forward from behind, with the free leg crossing the tracing to the front of the body. At this point both hands should be together to the front of the body, and, as for the three jump, you must push yourself up into the air going from the backward inside edge, up and over the toe rake as you leave the ice (see diagram).

It is important to keep the left side of the body in front and not allow the skating side of the body to swing around. Your hips and shoulders should be kept level at all times. Your body will rotate before the take-off as the backward inside edge gets stronger. You should not turn your body to

help rotate the jump – this is known as cheating!

Once you are in the air, the position for the flight and rotation is the same as for the waltz jump (see diagram). During the jump, try to keep your arms to the front of the body. You should feel relaxed and comfortable during the jump – always avoid feeling heavy. As you jump, your head should be held high and your shoulders kept down. You must always jump using the power in the lower part of the

The take-off.
ing the free leg
d arm forward
gether as the
ke-off lifts over
e toe rake.

3. Turn a very strong
three turn toward
the **outside of the
curve** and stop fully
the rotation with the
**left side of the
body pushed
forward, the right
side back**.

2. Step from
**backward outside
to forward
outside edge.**

1. The preparation
should always be on
a **backward
outside edge**.

body and not use the power in the upper body. The upper
body should give you the required control to rotate smoothly
and correctly.

The landing and exit sections are again very similar to
those of the waltz jump (see diagram). The landing must be
on a backward outside edge, with the toe rake touching very
quickly as you land before gliding onto the outside edge.

If you have not jumped high enough or you have

"pulled" the jump around, the landing will not feel very
comfortable and you should practice even more the three
turn section of the jump as this is very important.

Many skaters when learning the Salchow will be tempted
to "wrap" the free leg around the skating leg on take-off.
This is wrong and should be avoided. The free leg should
move forward and be slightly turned in, and not be too close
to the skating leg.

The Double Salchow

The double Salchow is rather like an Axel but it has a backward take-off. The take-off is the same as for the single Salchow and it has one-and-a-half revolutions in the air. The take-off edge is a backward inside edge.

Rather like the Axel, the single Salchow and the loop jump – as well as the backward outside upright spin – should be practiced until under control before attempting the double Salchow.

The major difference between the single and the double is that you will find yourself wanting to rush the double Salchow and will nearly always swing the jump around. Enormous control is required to ensure that the take-off is very much under control. The most important point is *prior* to the take-off when you're standing on the backward inside edge. You must have all of the body weight over the skating leg, with the free side of the body firmly held back (see diagram).

As the skating knee bends and starts to release for the take-off, the free side of the body is brought through with the free leg and arm being taken into the air as the jump takes off. As the free leg is taken forward the body weight should be very quickly transferred from the skating leg onto the free leg. At this point both arms are snapped in and the free leg will be placed to the front (see diagram). As with all double jumps, the arms should then be opened very quickly and firmly before landing, and the landing should be held for as long as possible with the free leg behind.

When learning double jumps you might not always land fully rotated to backwards, but it is a good habit to always land on one foot and complete the rotation on the ice by turning a three turn. It is bad practice to land on two feet or allow the body to collapse while in the air. Try to hold the body firmly in the air and avoid falling over when possible.

Practice off-ice as much as possible, particularly the pulling in and out of the arms during all jumps.

6. The **landing and exit** position.

5. The **flight and rotation stage**, shoulders and hips in line.

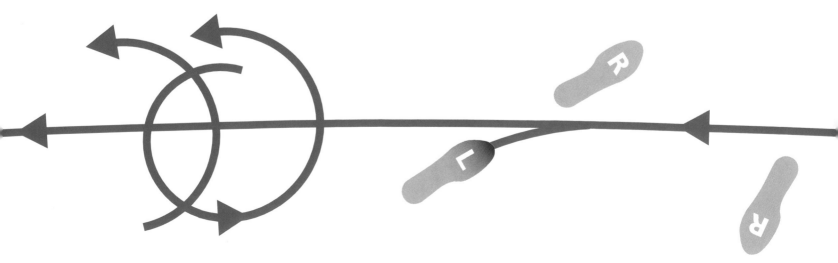

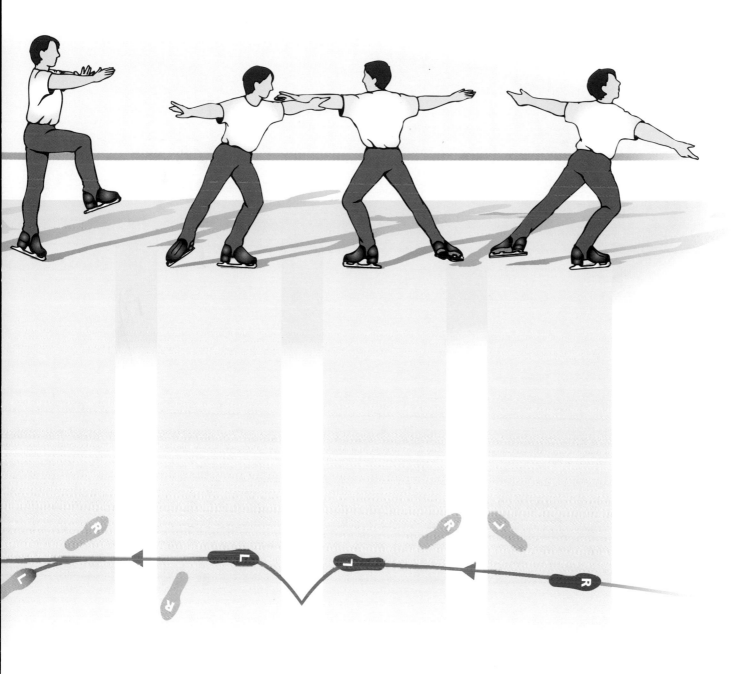

4. As you thrust **into the air toward the outside of the circle**, you will find the free leg is taken forward on a small arc passing away from the skating leg. Try to avoid any swinging around.

3. Backward inside edge, bending strongly to give more height.

2. The left side of the body is forward, in order to avoid swinging the body around.

1. As for the single.

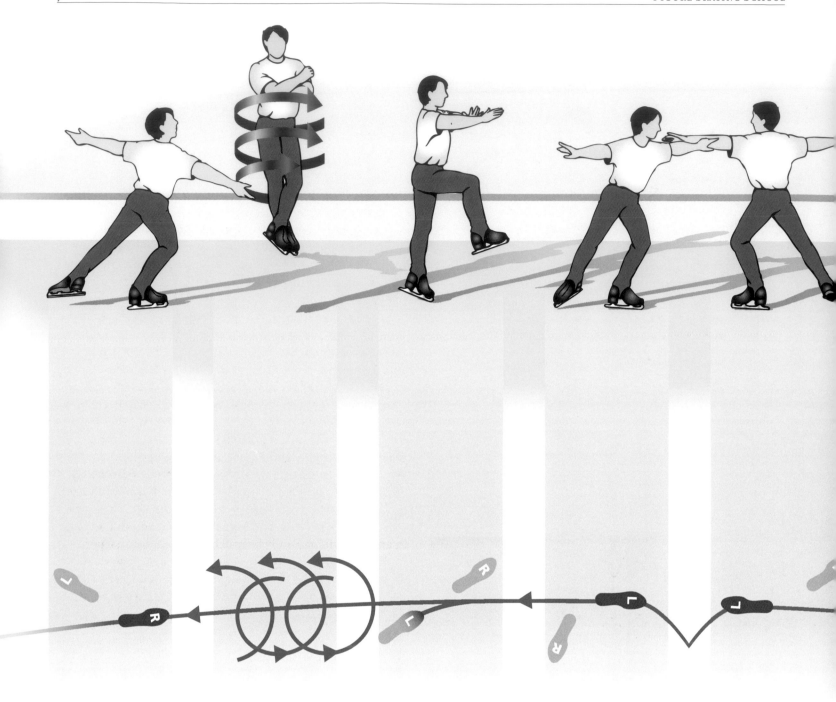

6. The landing. As always the toe rake touches the ice first and is then followed by the backward outside edge.

5. The rotation is created by a very strong pulling-in of the arms and crossing the feet as shown. (Never wrap the free leg around the skating leg.)

4. As for the double, the free leg will be brought through to the front a little closer to the skating leg this time. The **take-off is from the toe rake**, jumping toward the outside of the circle.

3. After the three turn look toward the left arm, and then press the right side of the body back.

2. Stepping to forward on **outside edge, to the outside of the circle.**

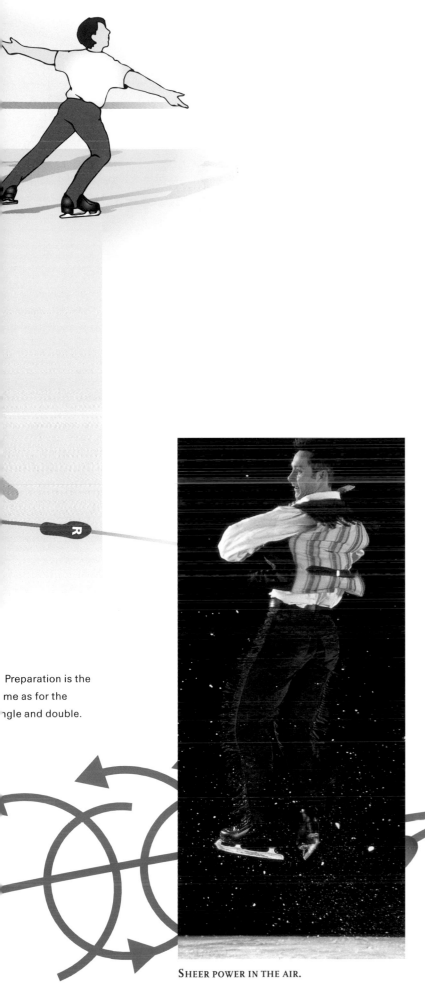

The Triple Salchow

As with all the triple jumps, mastery of the *doubles* is essential first. Your coach will know exactly when you are ready to try a triple. Single, double, and triple Salchows are all very similar; the difference is the number of rotations required. The diagrams show the different stages of the triple and, as with the double, complete control of the backward inside edge before the take-off is required.

The free leg movement on the take-off for the triple Salchow is slightly different from that of the single and the double. On a single Salchow the free leg moves through in a large curve to the front of the body and out of the circle. On the double, the movement is a little smaller and the leg does not move so far away from the body. On the triple the free leg is brought rather close to the skating leg on the take-off to allow for a quicker transfer of body weight and therefore a speedy transfer of weight from the take-off leg to the free leg to achieve the rotational position. The actual take-off will require more power than the double. The pull-in and-out will naturally be much stronger and sharper.

The landing is as for the double, although, as with all triples, it is a requirement that you be very much stronger in the back and the abdominal muscles to hold the pressure of so much rotation.

Preparation is the
me as for the
ngle and double.

SHEER POWER IN THE AIR.

The Toe Loop

The toe loop is sometimes called the cherry flip. Like the jumps we've already seen, this can be performed as a single, double, triple, or even a quadruple! In this section the single toe loop will be dealt with. This jump is the first jump that you will learn that uses the free leg and toe rake to assist the take-off. This is called a "toe-assisted" jump.

Remember that when you learn a single jump it is usual for you to move on to try the double and perhaps even the triple one day, so learning the single jumps correctly is very important.

1. The approach is from a **forward inside edge on the left leg**.

2. Change feet and skate a **forward inside three turn**.

The Single Toe Loop

The preparation for the toe loop is commonly skated starting with a forward inside three turn. Start on the inside edge of the left foot with your free leg extended in front. Bring your feet together, placing the heels together ready to change feet, moving slightly to the right and onto your right foot. As you change feet, bend both legs very strongly in order to push from the left leg onto the right. After changing feet, stand in a basic forward inside edge position with your free leg extended behind and your left arm in front (see diagram). While gliding, rise from the skating knee in order to turn a forward inside three turn. Your free leg should remain extended during the turn. Following the three turn, you should be skating on a backward outside edge with the free leg behind and the free arm in front (see diagram). You should practice this position to learn control of the hips and shoulders. The inside three turn can be easily swung out of control, making the take-off very difficult.

Once you have mastered the inside three turn you are ready to take off. After the turn your skating knee should bend very strongly as you reach back with the free leg. The toe rake of the free foot should touch the ice directly in line with the skating foot. The free foot should not twist or drop at this point. Your body weight should be maintained over the skating foot. As the skating foot is still gliding back toward the toe rake it must remain on the outside edge. It is very common for a skater to change edge and jump, wrongly, from the inside edge (this causes a waltz jump from the toe and not a toe loop). Or you might find that you are scratching with the skating toe rake. This will cause you to slow down and also skate the wrong take-off. The skating arm and shoulder should be back and the free arm and shoulder in front (see diagram showing the take-off).

The take-off is very important, as just before you take-off, your body weight should move back from the skating leg onto the toe rake of the free foot. As the skating leg moves through into the air, the lift comes from the "toe." Both arms follow the jump through and the position in the air is similar to the waltz and Salchow jumps (see diagram). As always, your head should be held high with the shoulders down.

You should land on a backward outside edge (see diagram). After the landing, a well-held position, as for all jumps, should be maintained (see diagram).

The toe loop is a very important jump, as it works with every other jump to make very important combination jumps.

After the three
a **backward**
side edge is
ted, with the free
extended behind
the free arm
ards the front.
position will fully
the rotation of
three turn.

4. The right leg will
bend strongly as
the left toe taps into
the ice. The **right**
backward outside
edge must continue
to glide back prior to
the take-off (often at
this point the skater
stops skating). The
body rotates to allow
the arms to move
around slightly
allowing the jump
to **take off very**
quickly from the
toe rake.

5. From the toe rake
the weight is then
pushed forward and
into the air **back**
onto the right leg.
The position in the
air is similar to
a waltz jump.

6. The landing
is as for all jumps.
Ensure that the left
arm is slightly to
the front.

1. As for the single.

2. As for the single. This inside edge should not be rushed, make sure that you are **standing firmly over the right leg**.

3. After the inside three turn **look forward toward the left arm**. This position should be practiced a great deal without jumping. Practising a backward outside "pivot" is a very good exercise for the toe loop take-off.

4. As the left foot taps the ice, the right foot must continue to glide on the **backward outside edge**.

The Double Toe Loop

This is based on the single toe loop. The take-off is from a backward outside edge assisted by the free leg when the toe rake is planted into the ice at the point of take-off. There are approximately one-and-a-half revolutions in the air and the landing is backward on an outside edge.

Once you have mastered the single and added the loop jump, you can attempt the double. As with all doubles the speed of rotation is very important and getting into the rotational position as quickly as possible is essential – but this must not be rushed. The take-off should be fully controlled (see diagram) with the left arm and shoulder placed to the front and the right arm and shoulder slightly back. Your body should be upright and the hips and shoulders in line. The right leg must bend very strongly as the left leg reaches back before the toe is planted into the ice. The left leg should be well extended as the toe is planted and the right knee will bend even more. As the toe touches the ice the right foot must be allowed to glide on and in front of the left toe, the extended left leg bends strongly as the right leg approaches. A common mistake is to stop the right foot from gliding as soon as the left toe touches the ice. This jump is a toe Axel and is not allowed.

As with all the double jumps, once you've performed the take-off, you must bring the arms in very quickly to enable the rotation to take place (see diagram). Hold the free leg to the front and as low as possible.

As always, the arms must open before the landing and the landing should be on a backward outside edge and held for as long as possible. On landing, the free leg should be taken back and extended.

The rotation for the double toe loop one-and-a-half turns in the air. The arms and free leg should always be close to the body but not too tight.

6. The landing should not be too far back on the skate. One of the major problems with toe-assisted jumps is jumping out of axis and then leaning back, giving a landing on the flat of the skate. Always make sure to **land with the toe first** and then quickly drop onto the **backward outside edge**.

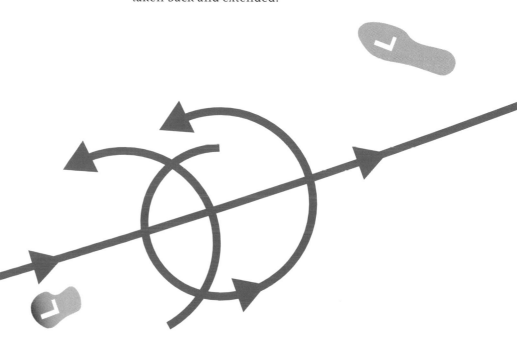

The Triple Toe Loop

The triple toe loop should be jumped rather like the double. If you follow the double toe loop instructions, the triple logically follows, but you'll need more power to gain more height and fast rotation. Working off ice will increase your awareness of the required positions. If there is a harness at your rink, use this with your coach to gain confidence. Having confidence, an excellent coach, and a really good basic technique will help you to achieve triple jumps.

Follow the diagrams to see exactly what goes on during a triple toe loop. During all jumps you should at all times keep your body upright and the hips and shoulders parallel to the ice. A dropped shoulder or hip could result in a nasty fall. Always control each stage of the jump, remember that *good* practice makes perfect – not just practice. The coach will act as your mirror, but if you can use a video camera as well this will allow you to see your own mistakes.

1. As for the double.

LEANING DURING THE TRIPLE.

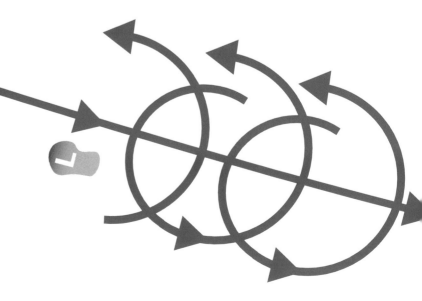

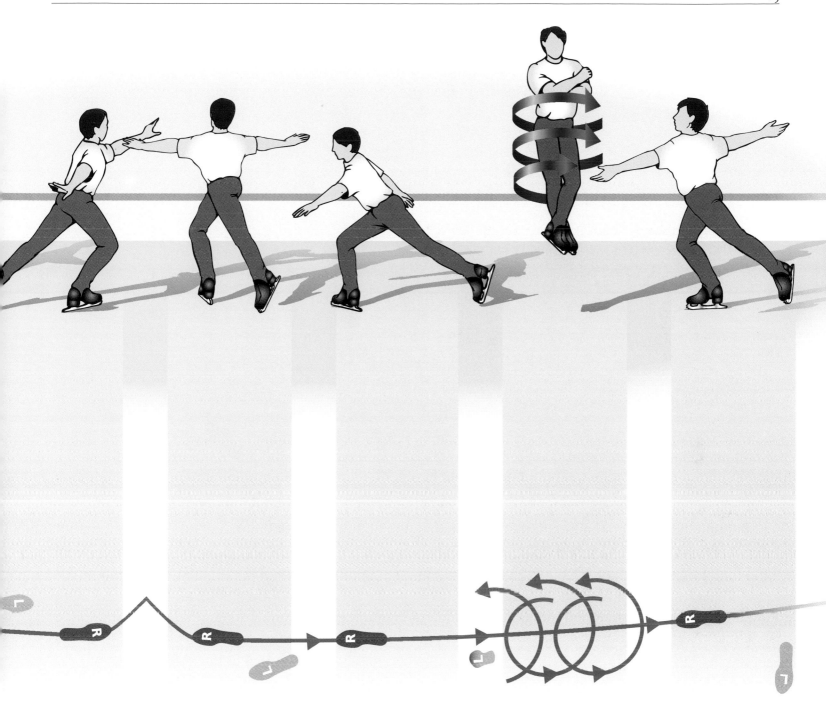

2. As for the double.

3. After the three turn, enormous strength, rhythm, and control are required before **tapping the toe rake into the ice**. Avoid allowing the shoulders to over-rotate after the three turn, or under-rotate. The shoulders and hips should face the front after the three turn.

4. The hips and shoulders will start to **rotate toward the outside of the circle** as the toe taps into the ice. As the toe taps, the jumping movement must be very smooth and continuous. The right leg moves back toward the tapping foot and then moves on into the air toward the outside of the circle.

5. A tight rotational position. Always keep the head up and the shoulders down. Your body should remain firm or it will break at the waist.

6. Open both arms and the free leg very strongly before landing. The arms and leg must open together.

The Loop Jump

The loop jump takes off and lands on the same foot with one full turn in the air. The take-off is from a backward outside edge with the landing, as for all jumps, also on a backward outside edge. When the single loop is mastered it can be developed into the double and eventually the triple. It is a jump that combines well and, like the toe loop, can be combined after all other jumps.

The Single Loop

The loop jump can be approached in several different ways. The easiest is by skating backward crosscuts on a large circle. This position is in fact the loop jump take-off position. You must stand on the right leg on an outside edge. Your left leg will be to the front directly in line with the right foot. The left foot should also be on an outside edge. The right arm, shoulder, and hip should be rotated back with practically all of your body weight over the right leg; a small amount of body weight may be on the left leg but very little. The left arm, shoulder, and hip should be forward, and the right knee should bend very strongly (see diagram).

Next comes the take-off. The right knee should bend a little more, allowing the right foot, still on outside edge, to turn slightly, making a hook-like tracing on the ice. As the right knee releases, the left leg must leave the ice as the right leg pushes you up into the air. Your right arm should come forward from behind to meet the left arm, which should still be in front of the body (see diagram).

When you're in the air your body will rotate once. Great care must be taken during the jump to make sure that hips and shoulders remain parallel. Avoid swinging the upper body around. As always, your head should be held high with both arms to the front of the body, not too tight or close to the body as this might cause over-rotation. Think of holding the pole as in previous jumps (see the diagram showing flight and rotation).

The landing and exit, as you'll see from the diagram, will be the same as for all jumps.

Try to combine several loop jumps. It's fun to try as many as possible.

READY TO LAND ONCE AGAIN.

3. After **one turn in the air**, the arms should open ready for the landing. **The landing** is also on the right leg.

2. The right leg should bend strongly. The **left leg leaves the ice and the right leg thrusts into the air**. Both arms are brought close to the body in order to help the rotation.

1. The preparation consists of **backward crosscuts on a circle**, followed by a nice **backward outside edge**. The body weight should be over the right leg, with the right side of the body back. The left side of the body is forward with the left leg touching the ice on backward outside edge. Very little body weight should be on the left leg.

4. The landing is on the same leg as for the take-off, on a very-well-controlled backward outside edge.

3. In the air, as for all double jumps, the arms must swiftly be brought close to the body. This will give **very smooth and flowing rotation**. A delay with the arms will cause the body to turn only very slowly and the complete rotations will not be made.

2. The take-off is taken from the backward outside edge followed by the toe rake. The toe rake touches the ice as the jump lifts into the air. Often skaters will tend to try to glide on the toe rake before taking off. This is wrong and will slow you down. Both arms will also help you to get lift as they are brought toward the body.

1. As for the single.
It is important to feel
relaxed at this point.

The Double Loop

The double loop is the first real double jump, with almost two revolutions in the air. The jump is as for the single, taken from a backward outside edge of the right foot, and the landing will be on the same foot. The double loop jump is a perfect example of the backward outside upright spin.

Timing plays an enormous part in all jumps but never more so than with the loops. Many of the greatest skaters have mistimed a loop jump and it has become, instead of a triple or a double, a single. Or, worse still, they have fallen badly on the take-off.

Stand firmly over the backward outside edge before the take-off. The right side of the body should be held back and the left side to the front, with the left leg placed directly in front of the skating foot. At the point of take-off the skating knee must bend very strongly as the whole body is then pushed up into the air with the left leg leaving the ice just before take-off. The left side of the body should be kept in front and not allowed to swing around behind the body. Often the left arm and shoulder will swing wildly back behind the body. This movement will throw you completely out of the body's axis and you could fall.

Once you're in the air, the arms must be brought in very quickly to allow a very speedy rotation. The free leg should be kept in front and on this jump the feet should cross, allowing the left foot to be kept very low and crossed next to the right foot. This will also help the rotation (see diagram). For the landing, the arms must be released and the left leg lifted out of the crossed position and held to the front, allowing for a clean landing on the right foot. The free leg should be taken behind only after the landing and held – as for all landings.

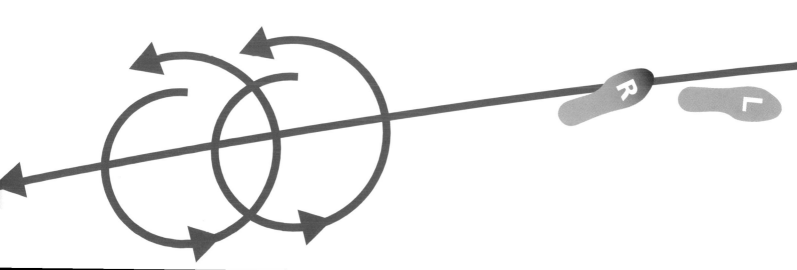

4. The landing must open strongly. Always open the arms before landing. If you land with the arms still closed the jump will continue to rotate. Always open the arms and the free leg together before you land.

3. The position in the air is as for the double and must have a sharper pull of the arms. The free leg and foot should be **neatly crossed and as close as possible to the right leg and foot**.

2. As with the double a **very strongly bent skating knee prior to the take-off** will give you additional height when the knee is released. It is very important to keep the shoulders and hips parallel during the take-off and not allow the free leg to swing wide and around. Be sure to keep the free leg at all times in front and slightly crossed.

1. More speed will be required for the triple loop. Most skaters wait for a very long time before taking-off. It is during this period that the skater will often wind up the body so much that the jump is no longer possible. Always feel comfortable over the **backward outside edge** and avoid waiting too long before taking-off.

The Triple Loop

The triple loop is possibly the hardest of the triples. Like the double loop, the triple requires enormous control of the backward outside take-off edge. All the work spent doing the backward outside spin will be of great importance to you for this one. The entry is as for the double. On the preparation edge, skaters will quite often wind themselves up so much that instead of jumping they fall over before the take-off. Avoid "winding up" too much. The position should feel comfortable and you should try to relax as much as possible before the take-off, feeling strong but not tight. Keep the shoulders down and the head up.

If the wind-up is too great, the body weight will fall back toward the heel of the skate and you will not be able to take the weight forward for the take-off. Always remember that all jumps actually take off from the toe rake. That means that this is the last part of the blade to leave the ice (not the heel). All landings will also be on the toe rake first, followed very quickly by the running edge. This follows the same principles as for jumping on dry land, whereby the feet roll forward to allow the toes to leave the floor last, then touch the floor first on landing, before allowing the remainder of the feet to contact the floor.

The triple loop follows the same principles as the double, but the speed of rotation is the important part of the jump. Landing is as for all jumps.

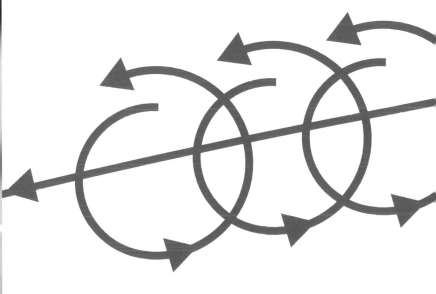

THE FOOT SHOULD BE CROSSED WHILE ROTATING IN THE AIR.

The Flip

The flip (or the toe Salchow) is another "toe-assisted" jump rather like the toe loop. The flip has one full rotation in the air and, of course, can be jumped as a single, double, or even a triple. The basic principles apply to all jumps and a good single jump should, with good coaching and lots of hard work and patience, develop into a double and even a triple if you are very talented.

The Single Flip (or Toe Salchow)

The flip is generally taken from a left forward outside three turn, or an inside open mohawk, leaving you backward on the left leg, skating a backward inside edge. This position should be practiced over and over in order to gain complete control of the rotation. It is very easy to turn to backward and have no control over the backward inside edge. As you turn to backward you must fully "stop" the rotation.

The left side of your body should be forward with the right side back. You should be looking toward your left hand and your right leg should be extended well behind with the toe pointing down, ready to "tap" the ice. Your back should be straight and, although the right leg is stretching back, you must be sure to stand fully over your left leg. The left leg must at this point bend very strongly as you are about to take off (see diagram).

To take off, the left leg should bend even more and, as the right toe taps the ice, the left leg continues to glide back to meet the right foot. At the same time the left leg is starting to push up and transfer the body weight onto the right leg. As the feet draw closer together both knees should bend even more in readiness for the take-off. This happens very, very quickly. When both feet are nearly touching, you should thrust into the air with the right leg assisting the take-off – rather like a pole vaulter jumping up and over a bar (see diagram).

As you lift up, the left leg transfers all of the body weight onto the right leg and while in the air you should adopt a loop jump position (see diagram).

The landing for the flip and the exit positions are the same as for all jumps.

5. The landing will be on a backward outside edge on the right leg.

4. One full turn must be completed in the air.

3. The take-off is from the toe of the right leg. As the toe taps the ice the left leg should bend even more as the left foot glides quickly back to the right. At the same time the jump is pushed into the air and the arms close toward the body.

2. Turn a **forward outside three turn**. Still skating in the same direction, make sure that you are on a backward inside edge with the left side of the body in front and the right side of the body back. This position will stop the rotation of the three turn. The right leg will be reaching back as far as possible.

1. The single flip has one full rotation in the air and is taken from a **backward inside edge**. The preparation is from a forward outside edge on the left leg. Keep the edge as straight as possible. It should not have a great deal of curve. On the left leg always stand with the left arm in front and use the right leg to push with.

The Double Flip

The double flip has two full rotations in the air. Like the single, it is a toe-assisted jump and has a backward take-off from an inside edge. The single flip should be practiced with a loop jump to give an understanding of the amount of rotation involved and the importance of good control.

All double and triple jumps require you to have enormous control of the arms, legs, head, shoulders, hips, back, and body weight. It is only when all of these are under control that the jump will be a well-controlled one.

The double flip starts in the same way as the single. In order to jump as high as possible, you must bend very strongly and know just how far back to take the body weight from the left leg and onto the right foot during the take-off. If the weight goes too far back, you'll lean back during the jump and land on the heel of the skate and almost certainly fall over. If the weight does not go far enough back, you'll lean forward and land too far forward on the toe. So you must be in your axis (an imaginary straight line running through the body). If the axis can be maintained, you will rotate quickly, efficiently, and safely and be able to perform excellent jumps.

Follow the instructions for the single, and, on the take-off, as with all doubles, snap your arms in and allow the left foot to cross in front of the right foot, leaving both legs extended in the air. Before landing, open the arms and take the free foot out of the crossed position and lift it slightly to the front.

A good take-off will ensure that the free leg does not wrap highly around the skating leg. This mistake is unsightly and is the sign of a poor take-off. Often, a skater has perhaps rushed from singles to doubles and the result is a poor take-off technique. As always the landing should be held on a backward outside edge for as long as possible.

6. The landing should be held for as long as possible on a **very strong backward outside edge**. Avoid allowing the landing edge to curl around making a very small curve; the landing should be a very strong, long curve (think straight).

5. As for all double jumps the **position in the air** is exactly the same.

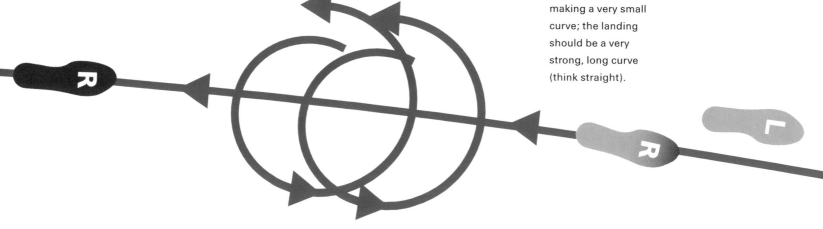

. The weight is transferred very quickly from the left to the right.

3. During **the take-off** the body axis must change from being over the left leg to being over the right leg. This happens as the left leg moves back to the right leg during the take-off.

2. As for the single. After the three turn you must **stand in your axis over the left leg**. Leaning too far forward or too far backward will also introduce many problems in the jump.

1. As for the single.

The Triple Flip

Follow the instructions for the double flip, and refer to the diagrams for the correct positions.

The triple flip is a jump with three full rotations in the air. The take-off is from a backward inside edge and the landing is, as always, on a backward outside edge. As with the double, the toe assists the take-off and, again, great attention should be paid to this part of the maneuver.

The take-off diagram shows the final position *before* take-off. The triple flip will land as for all jumps.

6. A strong landing is required as for all triple jumps.

5. The **rotational position** should be very tight as for all triple jumps. Remain very tall throughout the jump.

RUDI GALINDO IN TIGHT ROTATIONAL POSITION, MID-AIR.

The weight is transferred very quickly from the left to the right.

3. The **position after the three turn should be fully checked** before jumping.

2. As for the double.

1. As for the double.

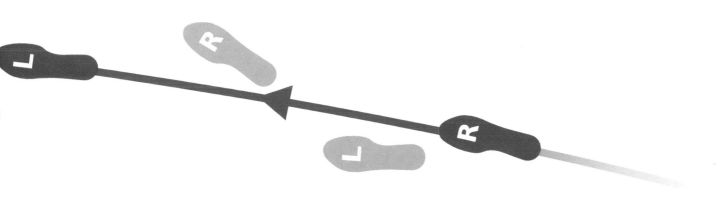

The Lutz

So far we have dealt with moves that all jump and rotate in the same direction as the take-off edge. The lutz, however, is the only jump that rotates against the take-off edge. Jumping against the take-off edge can lead to various problems with the lutz, and one of the major problems associated with it is the change of edge from the outside to inside.

The lutz must take off from a backward outside edge. It is also a toe-assisted jump – like the flip and the toe loop – and has one full rotation in the air.

The Single Lutz

The preparation is taken from back crosscuts skated in the reverse direction. You should stand on your left leg, on a backward outside edge, with your left arm, hip, and shoulder back, and your right leg, arm, hip, and shoulder to the front. Your head should be facing to the front looking toward your right hand.

As the curve continues, slowly start to move the arms and shoulders as you take the free leg from the front to the rear, all the time making sure that you are still on the outside edge. This movement makes a very good exercise. Your skating leg should bend very strongly as the free leg is taken back in readiness to tap into the ice (as in the flip). Your head should still be to the front (see diagram for preparation). As the free leg is taken back, it is important to keep your hips and shoulders parallel. Never lift your right hip and shoulder.

As the backward outside edge continues to proceed, the right foot will tap into the ice as the left skating leg continues, very quickly, to glide back toward the right foot. As the feet almost touch, the left leg thrusts into the air from the outside edge, and, as this happens, the body weight moves back onto the right leg and the right leg also thrusts into the air. The rotation is to the left, against the natural direction of the edge (see diagram).

Many skaters, when learning the lutz, will actually try rotating to the right, as this seems more natural. The flight and rotation stage of the jump are the same as for all the previous jumps, as you'll see from that part of the diagram.

In the air, your right leg should be extended underneath with the left leg to the front and slightly bent. Crossing your feet is not required for any single jump. Your arms should be directly to the front of the body, slightly curved, and a small distance from the front of the body. A tight arm position is not essential at this stage. As always, you should avoid feeling uncomfortable. Your shoulders must feel at ease and down, never hunched or strained, and your head should be held high.

The landing and exit positions are as for all jumps.

1. The lutz begins on a **backward outside edge** on the left leg skating in a clockwise direction. The left arm should be in front and the right arm slightly back.

he **right leg is wly taken back** the right leg ts to bend. The s and shoulders still in the same ition. The hips uld remain in line the shoulders.

3. As the right leg reaches further back the **left knee bends greatly**. As with the flip, the body must remain in axis at this point. The most important point with the lutz is remaining on the backward outside edge. Your body weight must remain over the left side of the body and well into the circle.

4. As the toe taps into the ice the left skate will **continue to travel back toward the right leg** (still on outside edge). As the left leg moves back, so does the axis as it transfers onto the right leg. At the same time the body thrusts into the air. Keep the body as still as possible. There should be little or no change of the arms, hips, and shoulders. The body will rotate to the left, against the natural direction of the edge.

5. In the air rotate as for all jumps. The lutz, however, rotates against the outside take-off edge, but once in the air the rotation is the same.

6. The **landing** is as for all jumps.

The Double Lutz

The lutz is the only jump that rotates in a counter-rotational direction; all other jumps rotate in the same direction as a three turn. This makes the lutz very difficult and can lead to the big mistake of changing edge from outside to inside before the take-off. This mistake leads to large deductions by judges in tests and competitions. The double lutz, like the single, starts from a backward outside edge (see diagram). The other rules, too, are the same as for a single, and of course it is highly recommended that you practice the lutz with the loop jump in combination, as well as with the backward outside upright spin.

The double lutz has two full rotations in the air and the arms should be pulled in closely toward the body at the highest point of the jump. As the lutz is toe-assisted, the way in which you transfer weight on the take-off is very important, to ensure that you remain in axis.

The free foot needs to be crossed closely during the jump (see diagram), and the landing should be well held.

1. As for the single.

MIDORI ITO IN A SPECTACULAR SPIRAL POSITION THAT DEMONSTRATES THE SKATER'S FLEXIBILITY.

. As for the single.

3. As with the single lutz, it is most important that you remain **on the outside edge** throughout the preparation and also the take-off.

4. On the double lutz more thrust will be required to gain maximum height. As you tap the right toe into the ice **the extended right leg will bend** as the body weight is absorbed into the leg and the axis starts to transfer.

5. The rotational position should always be firm but comfortable. Avoid hunching your shoulders in order to achieve extra rotation. It is only the pull of the arms that will give totally uninterrupted, smooth rotation.

6. The landing.

The Triple Lutz

The triple lutz is known and recognized for being the jump that has the very long backward outside take-off edge. Today this is no longer the case: the lutz for those competing at championship level should be attempted after a step sequence. This makes the jump much harder but may sometimes help to get rid of any change of edge. The fact that step edges are short can help to allow you to jump the lutz without having time to change edge.

Often the change of edge occurs because you have allowed your body weight to be transferred from the outside edge to the inside edge. To keep the body weight over the outside edge, ensure that the counter-rotation is maintained during the preparation. If this is lost, the body weight will change and then a change of edge will occur. Counter means *against*. This rotation is difficult to maintain because it is *against* the natural direction of the circle. All skaters should practice counter turns both forward and backward to improve their feeling for and understanding of them.

Follow the instructions for the single and double lutz, and study the diagrams. And remember: it is good height and the speed of rotation that are really important.

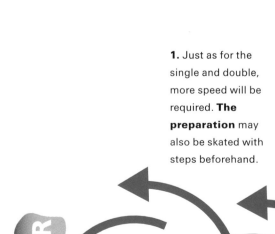

1. Just as for the single and double, more speed will be required. **The preparation** may also be skated with steps beforehand.

SURYA BONALY
OF FRANCE,
A GREAT SKATING
PERSONALITY.

. Great care
must be taken
not to anticipate
the rotation and
therefore lean away
from the circle. This
will lead to a large
change of edge.

3. As the right leg
moves back and the
left leg bends the
**right leg must be
placed directly in
line with the left
leg**. It should not be
allowed to swing
wide or pull back
into the circle.

**4. Reach even
further back than
on the double** as
the toe taps into
the ice, giving more
leverage as the jump
lifts into the air. As
you reach further
back the transfer of
the body axis is
greater than on the
double. Always
avoid moving the
axis too far back as
this could lead to a
fall on the landing.

**5. The rotational
position** is exactly
the same as for all
triple jumps.

**6. A very strong
landing** is required
on all triple jumps,
and a solid landing
is essential when
you are combining
the lutz with either
the toe loop or the
loop jump.

10. Exit.   **9. Landing.**   **8. Rotation.**

7. Following the landing the **left leg is taken back** and the toe loop is executed in exactly the same way as for a normal double toe loop.

6. The opening is the most important part of any combination. Here, the left leg is taken forward as the arms open. The left arm must also be taken forward. If this was to be a triple-flip double-loop combination, the free leg and arm must stay to the front and the loop jump would then be jumped as for a normal loop jump.

5. Rotation as for all triple jumps.

4. As for the flip.

Combination Jumps

Combining jumps is a very important aspect of jumping today. All jumps combine well when followed by either the toe loop or the loop jump. (It is also possible to place several jumps together and skate small steps or hops in between, although not classed as an official combination.)

During a combination, both jumps are skated in the normal way. For a combination with a loop jump, the free side of the body must be kept forward after the first jump in order to take off in the correct loop jump position. When combining a toe loop, the free side is taken behind to jump the toe loop in the normal way.

On a combination jump, the landing and take-off must be on one foot. You must never place your free leg on the ice between jumps and never rotate between jumps. Quite often a skater will land the first jump badly and will not be able to jump the second. It is very important to maintain good speed throughout the combination, as this will allow the second jump to be skated with more ease.

Landing the first jump with very-well-controlled arms is most important. If the first jump is landed with the free arm and shoulder back, it will be almost impossible to skate the second jump. Always ensure that the first jump lands with the free side of the body well in front. This will help to stop the rotation and allow a smooth take-off for the second jump.

The diagrams will help you understand the link between the first and the second jumps. (The illustration shows the triple flip, double toe loop.)

2. As for the flip.   **1.** Entry as for the flip.

As for the flip, **the entry should be very fast but not rushed**. On combination jumps try to keep the first jump long allowing the speed on the landing to give you length and time for the second jump. For the second jump you should try to jump higher than the first.

SPINS
GENERAL PRINCIPLES

Spinning on ice for many is the most beautiful part of figure skating. From the basic positions an almost unlimited number of combinations are possible and, when well done, can attract more attention than triple and quadruple jumps. The longest spin ever recorded was by a Swiss skater, Nathalie Krieg. She held an uninterrupted spin for 3 minutes and 22 seconds. This has been recorded in the Guinness Book of Records.

Spins all have the same basic principles and when these are understood, with lots of hard work, and under the guidance of an expert coach, you should be able to spin with great control.

The spinning principles are:

1   The Preparation.

2   The Entry.

3   The Spin.

4   The Exit.

Let's look at each section separately.

The Preparation

The preparation for any spin is very important. It is the point where you will wind your body up, ready to unwind and start the spin. The most common preparation starts with backward crosscuts in a clockwise direction. The circle should be rather small to start with. After several crosscuts skated in the normal way, the last crosscut should be held while the body "winds up" by standing on a very strong backward inside edge on the right leg and bringing the left side of the body forward and pulling the right side fully back. Your head should look over your right shoulder and your left leg should be strongly stretched out of the circle (see diagram). This position should be held until a full circle has been skated on the right leg.

The Entry

The entry into any spin is crucial if the spin is to work well. From the above preparation position you should remain in the wind-up position but take the left leg from its stretched position outside the circle and step to forwards onto an outside edge, stepping toward the center of the circle that has already been skated. Once you have stepped toward the center of the circle (you should never step out of it!) the arms should stay in the same position as during the preparation. Often a skater will change position before stepping to forwards and will then step out of the circle, leading to many problems.

As you step to forwards, the entire left side of the body should be pushed forward, and your head will rotate to look to the center of the circle. What follows will decide if the spin is to work well or not.

Remaining on a very strongly bent left knee with the left arm, shoulder, and hip pushed forward and the right side of the body back, you should skate a very strong forward outside edge, holding the right leg back all of the time. Do not allow the right leg to move forward at this stage. This outside edge will decrease in size due to the very strong knee bend and the positioning of the body weight toward

the center of the circle. As this edge continues to decrease in size you will start to slow down and come to a near standstill. As this happens, the right leg, which should still be held back, is brought forward very strongly on a large arc, pulling away from the body, then making you turn a very quick three turn. This three turn is unlike the three turn that you will have previously learned because you must try to spin on top of the three turn and not skate out of it, or else you will start to "travel" away from the center of the spin (see diagram).

Once the three turn has been performed you will be spinning on a backward inside edge. Your left leg should be still strongly bent and your right free leg extended to the side of the body with your arms held at about waist height, also stretched out to the side. Your body weight should be over the ball of the skate, never on the toe rake. A good spin should make no noise.

You should feel as though somebody were pulling your free leg and arms away from you while you are pulling them back in.

This entry is valid for all spins with some slight variations.

The Spin

Once the entry has been mastered it should be possible to develop any spin. All spins should be well controlled and centered: that is, not allowed to travel but remain on the spot. The following spins are the most common.

The Upright Spin

The Cross-toe or Scratch Spin

The Backwards Outside Upright Spin

The Sit Spin

The Parallel Spin

The Layback Spin

These spins can be combined to make very beautiful spins, such as a parallel spin changing to a layback spin, a change of feet to a sit spin, and then a cross-toe spin to finish. All spins have a change of foot position and are required in competition and test work.

The Exit

The exit from a spin, like a jump, should be well controlled and held for as long as possible to demonstrate good balance and command of the spin. The exit should look rather like a jump landing (see diagram).

The Upright Spin

The upright spin is the first spin that you will learn. It can then be developed into a cross-toe spin. The upright spin begins in the normal way with a good preparation and entry as described in the previous section. Once the entry has been completed, and you are spinning on a well-controlled backward inside edge, you must first slowly bring your free leg in toward the left leg at knee height. As this is happening, both arms should feel that they are getting stronger. They should certainly not feel loose, or the spin will not get any faster. The arms should then be slowly brought toward your chest. If this is being done correctly it will feel as though you cannot bring your arms in as they will want to pull away. The closer the arms are brought in the faster the spin will turn.

After as many turns as possible open your arms to slow the spin down. Lower the free leg toward the ice and change feet to exit on the right leg with the free leg stretched well back and strongly turned out.

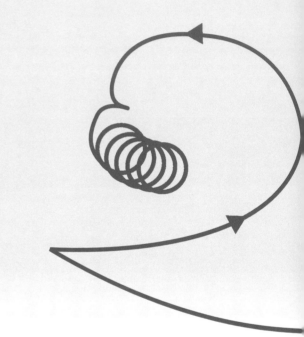

5. The diagram shows a **variation for the arms and a very closed free foot**, giving even more speed. The exit position will be on the right foot, rather like a jump landing.

4. Slowly allow both arms to be brought toward the body as the free leg is also brought in. This will **allow the spin to accelerate**. The spin should at all times be well centered.

3. When the three turn is turned the free leg should be brought forward around to the side, away from the left leg. Both arms should be well stretched out. **The spin is skated on a backward inside edge**, spinning on the ball of the foot.

The Cross-toe Spin

A cross-toe spin (or scratch spin) is almost the same as the upright but the free foot will be crossed in front of the spinning foot and slowly pushed down toward the ice until both feet are crossed. This will make you spin even faster.

The basic arm movement is to bring them both toward your chest slowly. However, there are variations on this. One is to bring both arms slowly above the head and stretch them upward (see diagram).

The resulting tracing on the ice should be a series of very small circles all on top of one another and in turn placed on top of the original three turn.

A CROSS FOOT SPIN.

2. Step to a **forward outside edge** toward the center of the already skated circle, keeping the left side in front. Then skate a **very long forward outside edge**, keeping the free leg well back until the left skate almost stops. Try to skate a number six on the ice as the edge gets deeper and deeper.

1. The basic wind-up position. This is skated on a backward inside edge after several backward crosscuts.

5. The final position. This should look like a jump landing.

4. The exit. Now open both your arms and take the left leg forward so that the rotation stops.

3. The spinning position. Notice that the arms are crossed close to the body and the feet are crossed at the ankles. This position will help you with all your jumps.

2. Once you have centered the spin, bring the **free leg and arms slowly toward the body.** This will then increase the speed of the rotation.

1. Skate a forward inside three turn on a very strongly bent skating leg. After the three turn you should spin on a **backward outside edge making sure the left leg is well extended** away from the body. Your weight should be on the ball of the foot.

The Backwards Outside Upright Spin

This one is as important as the upright spin. It will help you to combine all the basic spins, for example, change foot upright spin, change foot sit spin and so on. This spin will also give you a very good feeling for all jump rotations and should be mastered before attempting any double jump.

The entry can be made in several ways, the easiest being to skate a normal upright spin and then change feet onto the outside edge of the free foot and spin in the same direction as the first spin. This can be done several times, changing from one foot to another, first slowly and then gaining speed.

The diagram shows a skater entering from a forward inside three turn on the right foot. The skater bends very strongly and stretches the free leg well behind, and holds the free side of the body to the front. Because of the very strong knee bend the curve will be very deep and the skater will turn an inside three turn very quickly, but keep the free side of the body to the front and the free leg to the front, well extended, and pulling away from the body, creating resistance. While rotating, the skater must remain on the backward outside edge, spinning over the original three turn. The free leg and arms are then slowly brought in toward the body as for the normal upright spin, leaving the skater in a very tight position with the feet crossed and the arms tightly closed to the front of the body. The exit should, once again, look rather like a jump landing.

A CATCH-FOOT SPIN IN ACTION.

5. Rise on the same leg and then **exit by changing feet**. The exit is as always on a very strongly bent skating knee with a very extended and turned-out free leg.

4. While spinning **keep your head and back upright** and place your arms close to the body. This will help you to gain more speed.

3. As the free leg is brought around toward the front and the three turn is executed, you must **lower yourself almost to ice level** and allow the right leg to come in toward the left leg.

2. Stepping to forward going towards the center of the circle.

The Sit Spin

The sit spin should be learned in the same way as the upright spin.

This time, instead of bringing the free leg toward the body, it should remain stretched while the left leg bends as low as possible to bring you down almost to ice level. While bending down, you must keep your head up and your back upright. On the way down, you should bring your extended free leg in toward the skating leg and your arms should also be brought in close to the body to gain speed.

Various arm positions are possible (see diagram).

The basic wind-position as for upright spin.

A DRAMATIC END TO A SKATING PROGRAM.

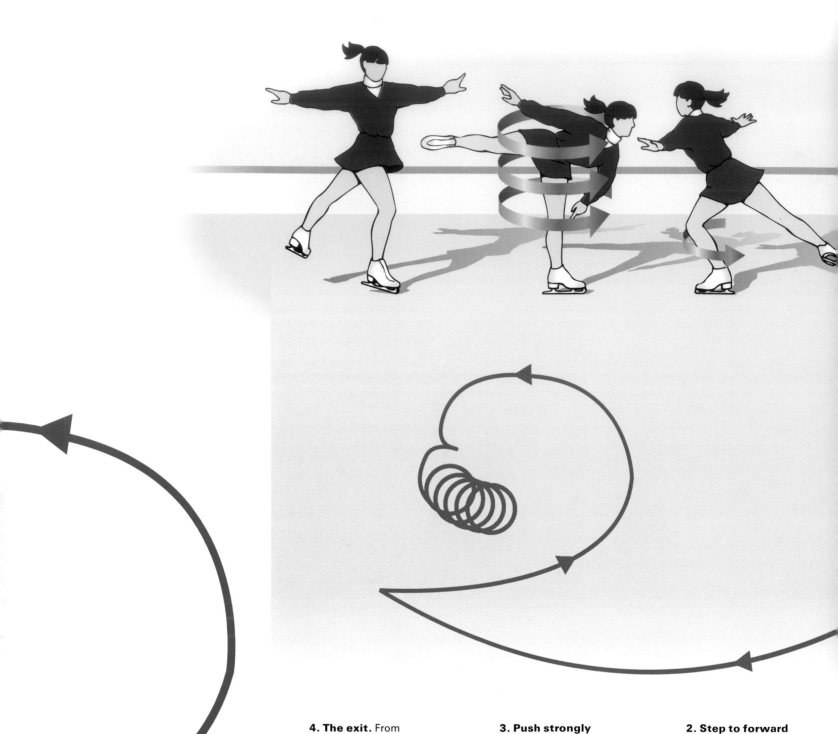

4. The exit. From the parallel position come up into an upright spinning position and then change feet in time for the exit.

3. Push strongly into the spin, leaving the free leg behind as the curve is skated and the three turn executed. Lift the free leg behind into the spiral position and then straighten the left leg very quickly. Your arms may be positioned in many different ways. Try to spin as far back on the skate as possible, and avoid leaning forward.

2. Step to forward just as for the upright and sit spins.

The Parallel Spin

The parallel spin should look like a spinning spiral or arabesque.

The preparation and entry are the same as for all of the other spins. The main difference with the parallel spin is that the free leg does not come through to the front, but remains behind you while it lifts into the parallel position. Of the three basic spins this is the hardest to learn, as it is difficult to find the exact spinning point on the blade. Often, skaters will fall forward over the toe rake as the body pushes forward into the parallel position.

Lots of practice will be required with the parallel spin. You should also be very flexible, as your leg should go as high as possible. The parallel spin is the slowest of all spins. Gaining speed is very difficult, therefore an excellent entry position is very important (see diagram).

ntry as for the

ght and sit spin.

ILLYA KULIK SHOWS MASCULINE POISE AND GRACE.

The Layback Spin

The layback spin is perhaps the most attractive spin. Both male and female skaters may do this spin and there are many variations on the layback, ranging from a simple head-back position while spinning, to a full layback with the free leg held and extended above the head, known as a Biellmann spin.

The basic layback spin has the same entry as for an upright spin. Finding your balance first is the important thing. Trying to lay (or, strictly, lie) back while traveling is very dangerous, so make sure that your upright spin is very good and well centered before trying the layback. From the basic "open" upright spinning position with a strongly bent skating leg, the arms should be taken to the front of the body to create a curve. The free leg, still extended, should then be taken behind and held as high as possible. At this point you should slowly start to lie back, starting from the hips and working up to the head. As you lie further back the arms can be lifted higher into the air (see diagram).

At first you will feel very dizzy as you face the ceiling and your eyes start to watch it go round. This is normal, and with lots of practice it will go away.

There are many variations on this basic position. Try this and some different positions off the ice. The choice is endless, with lots of arm positions and free leg positions. You may even try to hold the free foot blade with the free arm and draw it toward your head while spinning. Always attempt new moves under the watchful eye of your coach.

1. Follow the instructions for a normal upright spin and then gradually **take the layback position**, being very careful not to lean back too far at first.

A LAYBACK SPIN POSITION.

. The layback
osition.

THE "BIELLMANN" SPIN.

The Flying Spins

A flying spin is a cross between a jump and a spin; the jump will always take place first, followed by the spin. The most important factor when learning a flying spin is to understand that the position in the air is very important. For example, a flying (or jump) sit spin must fully show the sit position in the air before landing and then spinning in the sit spin position.

Flying spins must demonstrate great skill and control, because the spin that follows must not travel but must show good, controlled speed. The jumping position creates a very athletic look and is always very impressive when done well and at speed. It is recommended that skaters only learn flying spins when they have fully mastered all of the basic spins.

One flying spin must be included in the Short Program. This must be as per the current rules and regulations as laid down by the International Skating Union. The number of rotations that follow the "jump" are very important – currently a minimum of eight rotations must follow the flying position in the required spinning position.

The Flying Camel

The flying camel is the first of several flying spins you will learn. It is difficult, as are all of the flying spins, and will need lots of hard practice.

You should be flexible, as you will be required to jump high into the air with both legs extended and land in a camel/parallel position and spin for at least eight revolutions.

The flying camel is very dynamic and should be entered into in the same way as the parallel spin. The free leg during the entry to the spin will swing out wide from the body and start to draw a large circle in the air. As this is happening, the skating leg, which as always should be very well bent, will start to thrust into the air from the toe rake. The free leg continues to "fly" through the air while the jumping leg also pushes up behind into the air creating a "flying" position. You should keep both arms extended and your body parallel to the ice (see diagram).

The landing should be to the outside of the take-off curve and not inside. You should land on the toe of the right leg and very quickly start to spin on the backward outside edge as far back as possible on the blade. The momentum for the spin will come from the free leg, which will whip back as you land and give you lots of power. A weak free leg will give no power at all and the spin will be very short.

All flying spins should look very athletic and will require lots of off-ice work to achieve the correct positions.

One of the most common errors with the flying camel is to take off too late, leaving a three turn on the ice. This must be avoided. The take-off should be from a forward outside edge and over the toe, and not a backward inside.

5. Once you have landed try and spin as far back as possible on the backward outside edge. Avoid spinning on the toe rake. **Exit on the right foot on a backward outside edge.** Exit with speed and power.

4. The arms should be stretched out with the body kept flat. **As the right leg lands ready to spin the left leg should maintain its high position in the air**. The power in the left leg will start the parallel spin for you. As you land, the body should be perfectly held in a parallel position, the body and arms still.

3. The left leg, when it would otherwise turn a three turn to start spinning, must be **pushed up into the air behind you** and also allowed to swing wide.

2. The **right leg should swing around** very strongly away from the body in a very continuous movement. Keep the right leg high as it is coming through. Think of taking it over the barrier.

1. The entry is as for a normal parallel spin. The knee-bend must be very powerful as you are about to jump.

The Death Drop

The death drop is a combination of a flying camel and a sit spin. It is very athletic and requires great skill and courage.

The death drop starts as for a flying camel but with even more thrust and height, allowing the right leg to be brought forward, around, and as high as possible on the take-off. The left leg, having skated a very strong forward outside edge, will push up behind you and over the toe. The left leg must then thrust up into the air as high as possible above your head. At this point the right leg will be coming down ready for the landing on a backward outside edge. The left leg then quickly follows and a backward outside edge sit-spin position should be taken.

During the jump you should try to keep your back flat with your arms fully stretched. If your back is too high both legs will not go high enough behind and the jump will not look so impressive (see diagrams).

A really good death drop will be skated with lots of speed.

BONALY SHOWS HER GYMNASTIC SKILLS WITH A HANDSTAND DURING EXHIBITIONS.

7. Exit position.

6. After the sit spin **stand up on the same leg**.

5. The landing should be on a backward outside edge. As soon as the landing has taken place, turn very quickly, as the left leg drops down, and take a backward outside sit-spin position.

4. Your body should drop forward slightly to **allow the left leg to be pushed as high as possible into the air behind**. Maintain this position for as long as possible. Upon landing, the left leg should still be behind and in the air.

3. Thrust both arms and the right leg forward as the jump is pushed into the air.

2. Bend the left leg very strongly. Both arms should be behind the body, as will the right leg.

1. The death drop must be skated with speed. **Step forward onto the left leg on the outside edge.**

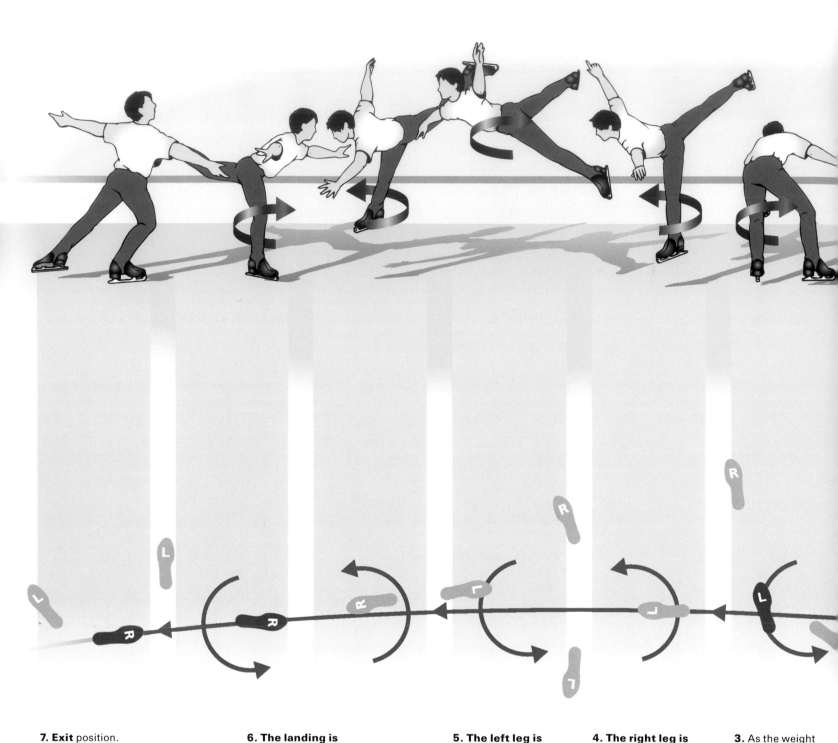

7. Exit position.

6. The landing is on the right leg on a forward inside edge. A forward inside three turn is quickly turned as the left leg is taken down and pushed back for the exit.

5. The left leg is then pushed up into the air, creating the butterfly position in the air.

4. The right leg is thrown into the air, the arms extend fully, and the back is brought up, but the legs must be higher than the back.

3. As the weight fully transfers over onto the left leg **the right toe must tap into the ice**.

Lower the body rther as the left n attempts to uch the right foot. the same time ace the left foot to the ice and rt to transfer the dy weight from e right to the left g (a little like an side spread-eagle sition).

1. The entry to the butterfly can be skated rather like a **backward outside upright spin**. Start on the right leg on an inside edge with the left arm forward.

The Butterfly

The butterfly is also a flying spin that is very impressive and athletic to see.

You should start as for a backward outside spin on a forward inside edge, but allow your body to move forward with the left arm reaching down toward the right foot, with the right arm slightly higher. At this point your body weight should shift from the right leg to the left leg, while you skate quickly backwards on both feet.

As the body weight transfers across from right to left, the right toe will catch the ice and start to push up into the air behind. The left leg then follows very quickly. Your back and head should then push up, too, with the arms extended, leaving you in a very beautiful position in the air.

The landing can be in a sit-spin position on the right leg or it can be combined with another butterfly (see diagrams).

A BEAUTIFUL BUTTERFLY JUMP.

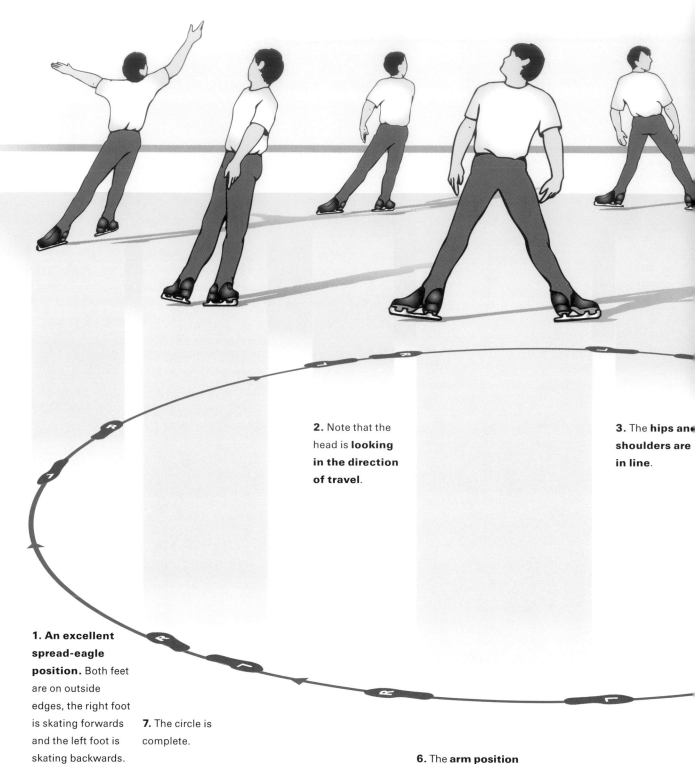

2. Note that the head is **looking in the direction of travel**.

3. The **hips and shoulders are in line**.

1. An excellent spread-eagle position. Both feet are on outside edges, the right foot is skating forwards and the left foot is skating backwards.

7. The circle is complete.

6. The **arm position** can be varied.

The Spread Eagle

The spread eagle is a very impressive movement that is skated with both skates on the ice at the same time. They can be skated on outside or inside edges and create a very large circle or part of a circle. The diagram shows a full-circle spread eagle on outside edges.

The outside spread eagle is the hardest to perform as you must be very open-hipped. Skaters with closed hips will find this movement almost impossible. They should work on the inside spread eagle, as this is a little easier but not so impressive.

The Spiral

Spirals can be skated forward, backward, on outside edges, and on inside edges right and left. A spiral is an attitude position with many variations.

The most important thing about the spiral is that the free leg should be at least as high as the skating hip. Variations on arm, head, and leg positions are allowed. You may even hold your free leg and assist it to go higher during the movement. A spiral should look attractive at all times.

4. Never allow the hips to stick out behind. **The body should be inclined into the circle**.

5. No wobbles are to be skated – just **a very smooth clean curve**.

The spread eagle should be approached skating forward on the left leg on an outside edge. The free side of the body should then be taken as far back as possible, allowing the right skate to touch the ice cleanly on the outside edge. During the spread the whole body should be facing outside of the circle (see diagram).

On an inside spread the body will be facing inside of the circle. The hips and feet do not have to turn out so much making it a little easier to perform.

KATARINA WITT DEMONSTRATES A SPIRAL.

Rules and Competition

The rules governing competitions and championships are very complex. They change on a fairly regular basis. The rules are established by the world governing body for ice skating, the International Skating Union. Various technical committees, formed by elected members from around the world, meet on a regular basis and decide the best way forward for the sport.

Rules change to keep abreast of the constantly changing world of ice skating. When a rule changes the rest of the world must also change. All championships, both national and international, as well as competitions, are all based on the same rule book.

Changes and modifications to rules will affect the way an event is judged and the contents of the various programs that are to be skated. Skaters, coaches and judges must all be aware of the changes and each national association is responsible for keeping everyone informed of any rule change.

Many of the rules concern deductions for mistakes made during a program. Putting a hand down after a jump, landing on two feet, lacking in rotation in a jump, falling over, not rotating sufficiently during a spin, or missing an element out altogether are just some of the areas that will lead to large deductions. Often a skater will accumulate many errors during a program – and, the more errors, the more deductions!

Marks range from zero to a perfect six with decimal points in between. For example, 0.8 or 2.7 or 5.8 are all marks that might be awarded. The perfect 6.0 mark means that no deductions have been made.

In free skating the judges award two sets of marks: the first will be for the technical content of the program, the second for the presentation. Often these marks can vary greatly. In major championships a panel of up to nine judges (always an uneven number) will sit and watch each performer and will award the two marks. During the event the judges must not speak to one another, but must award marks according to the difficulty of the program skated, and after all deductions have been made.

On the panel will be a referee and an assistant referee. They may not judge the event, but they must oversee the judging and make sure that all the judges are judging correctly and that the conditions for the skaters are perfect. If there are any problems the referee must deal with them. Sometimes the skater's music does not start, or skaters injure themselves during the competition. Occasionally, laces come undone. It is the referee who must decide what course of action to take.

Most skaters will start skating in a local club, take local club or rink grades, and then proceed on to national grades. National grades, or examinations, must be taken at different levels before you take part in the various competitions that are open to your age and grade. To participate in a national championship, you must first pass the required skating grade, then be of the required age for the championship, and then skate through any regional or selection round before taking part in the finals.

For those lucky enough to compete at a championship level, selection for international competition and championship might follow allowing you to travel around the world and be seen on television by millions of skating fans.

Most skaters dream of skating in the World Championships or the Olympic Games. Only very few achieve that goal. But there are many wonderful times to be had skating in club competitions, taking grades, working really hard for the next jump or spin, or just simply skating because it is something that you love doing.

Maybe one day your dream will come true.

HAPPINESS AND A FAREWELL AT THE END OF A SKATING PROGRAM.

Glossary of Terms

Axis An imaginary line running through the center of the skater, around which the skater rotates, jumps or spins.

Bracket Turn A counter rotated turn from either outside to inside or inside to outside edges, forwards to backwards or backwards to forwards. The cusp of the turn pointing to the outside of the circle, forming a bracket shape, hence its name.

Chassé A series of 2 steps, usually skated outside edge followed by an inside edge, while the free foot is simply lifted an inch or so above the ice and next to the skating foot without a strike.

Check or Check out This is a slight reversing of the hips and shoulders against an already existing rotation, as after turns or on landing jumps, in order to stop or lose unnecessary rotation.

Choctaw A step from forwards to backwards or backwards to forwards to opposite edges. For example, forward inside to backward outside. This causes the skater to change from one circle to another.

Circular Step Sequence A series of steps skated on a circle using the full width of the ice rink. Jumps may be no more than half a turn.

Contra-body This is a skating position where the body of the skater is in opposition. That is, with the hip against the opposite shoulder and arm, causing a tension and twist in the body.

Counter Turn This is a counter rotated turn to the same edge. For example, inside to inside or outside to outside edges. This causes the skater to skate into a new circle with this turn. Like a Bracket the cusp of the turn points to the outside of the starting circle.

Cross rolls A series of crossed steps from outside edge to outside edge. This causes the steps to be skated in a series of half circles.

Edge The curve a blade skates on the ice depending on the inclination, and weight distribution of the skater. These are either outside, inside edges, forwards or backwards. All steps and movements should be on clean running edges.

Free Foot or Leg This is the leg not on the ice.

Grind The term referred to when the skating blades are sharpened. A blade has several different grind depths according to the skater, weight, blades and discipline.

Inside Edge This is when the skater's weight is inclined to the inside of the circle and the inside of the skater's body or skating leg.

Lobe A pattern of two half circles joined together to create an S shape. A lobe may cover a small section of the ice or half of the ice surface. The lobe should be symmetrical.

Mohawk This is a step from forwards to backwards on the same edges and this causes the steps to keep you in the same circle.

Outside edge This is the curve skated by the skater when their weight is in the circle and to the outside of their body or skating leg.

Progressive Run A series of 2 steps or more consisting of an outside edge and where the inside edge is placed progressively or ahead of the other foot. Power is gained on each step.

Pattern The shape a series of steps or movements leaves on the ice.

Program A series of steps, movements, spins and jumps that shows off the skater's skills and virtuosity. Programs vary in time from 1-5 minutes according to standard and requirements.

Radius The curve or rocker running from the heel to the toe of the blade, allowing the skater to transfer their weight from the front to the back of the skate and therefore be able to turn etc.

Rocker Turn A turn from outside to outside or inside to inside either forwards to backwards or backwards to forwards. This turn is rotated into the circle.

Serpentine Step Sequence A series of turns and steps covering the full ice surface with a minimum of 2 lobes. The lobes must begin at one end of the ice surface and finish at the opposite end.

Skating Leg or Foot This is the employed leg that is on the ice.

Straight Line Step Sequence A series of turns and steps that must be skated along the full length of the ice rink. Jumps of not more than half a turn are permitted. May be skated corner to corner or end to end.

Stroke or Strike This is the movement when the skater pushes from one foot to the other, which causes a smooth weight change.

Toe Rake or Pick The front section of the blade comprising a number of jagged teeth allowing the skater to jump, spin and skate toe steps.

Index

PICTURE CREDITS
The publishers would like to thank Allsport
Photographic plc, International Sports Picture
Agency, 3 Greenlea Park, Prince George's Road,
London SW19 2JD, England, for supplying
photographs for the following pages: 2, 6-7, 8,
10, 11, 12, 13, 14, 15, 16-17, 19, 23, 32, 37, 38, 39,
49, 51, 52, 55, 58, 59, 60, 61, 62-63, 64, 65, 67,
71, 72, 79, 84, 86, 90, 96, 100, 102, 106, 107,
109, 111, 113, 115, 116, 120, 123, 124, 125, 126,
127, 128.
The photograph of Sonja Henie on p9 is
reproduced by kind permission of the Heni-
Onstad Kunstsenter, Høvikodden, Norway.